Commu

Yc

Way to
SUCCESS

Dale Carnegie Success Series titles
published by Manjul Publishing House

◆*Living an Enriched Life*
◆*Become an Effective Leader*
◆*How to Jump-Start Your (Next) Career*
◆*10 Steps to a More Fulfilling Life*
◆*Overcoming Worry & Stress*
◆*How to Have Rewarding Relationships,
Win Trust and Influence People*
◆*Life Is Short Make It Great*
◆*Embrace Change for Success*
◆*Resolve Conflicts in Your Life*

Communicating Your Way to SUCCESS

DALE CARNEGIE

MANJUL

Manjul Publishing House

First published in India by

MANJUL

Manjul Publishing House

• 7/32, Ansari Road, Daryaganj, New Delhi 110 002 - India
Website: www.manjulindia.com

Registered Office:
• 10, Nishat Colony, Bhopal 462 003 - India

The Success Series:
Communicating Your Way to Success by *Dale Carnegie*

This edition first published in India in 2018

Copyright © Dale Carnegie & Associates
Rights licensed exclusively by JMW Group Inc.
jmwgroup@jmwgroup.net

ISBN 978-93-87383-28-9

Cover Design by Trinankur Banerjee

This edition is authorised for sale in the Indian Subcontinent only.

Printed and bound in India by Thomson Press (India) Ltd.

CONTENTS

PREFACE

....

COMMUNICATION IS A
TWO-WAY STREET

There are four ways, and only four ways, in which we have contact with the world. We are evaluated and classified by these four contacts: what we do, how we look, what we say, and how we say it.

Dale Carnegie

These days, communication—what we say and how we say it—is a major factor of our success or failure. The great leaders of government, industry, and education are all skilled in their ability to communicate effectively with other people.

This skill is not necessarily inborn. Anybody who desires to can acquire it. All that is needed is will and determination.

Once we have improved our ability to communicate, we can more effectively present our ideas to our bosses, associates, customers, even our friends and family.

Imagine being able to communicate with more power and excitement. We can change a boring meeting into a dynamic, profitable one. We can inspire and motivate our associates to meet those deadlines and exceed our projected goals.

Much of day-to-day communication creates an opportunity for miscommunication and misunderstanding. Some of the language that is used might be easily understood within our own organization, but that jargon is often confusing for those outside our company or industry.

When we organize our thoughts and don't try to cover the entire range of a topic, we keep those listening to us on the same page because people like order and clarity. All professionals must be able to express their opinions clearly, concisely, and convincingly, especially in impromptu or unexpected situations. Those situations require courage, confidence, the ability to organize thoughts quickly, and the ability to express them in a coherent and persuasive way.

Communication is not a one-way street. It is not just the communicator giving a message to another party. To be effective it must be a two-way highway with feedback flowing from one party to the other on a continuous basis. The sender of the message must seek and receive feedback from the receiver. The communicator must be always assured that what is sent is understood and accepted by the receiver. To accomplish this, the sender must ask questions, observe what is observable and, if there are misunderstandings, correct them and assure that the corrections are understood. He or she must seek the acceptance of the communication by the receiver so that there exists a willingness to accomplish what is desired.

By following these fundamentals of good communication, not only will our messages get across more readily but also work will be accomplished with fewer errors and on time. Our people will be more efficient and happier, and we will be able to do our job as a manager with fewer problems and more satisfaction.

In this book, you will learn some strategies to improve both your oral and written communication—major steps toward becoming more successful in your job and in every aspect of your life.

You will learn how to perfect your oral communication skills from the day-to-day experience of talking one to one with another person—the art of conversation—to making public speeches to a large audience or presenting a report to members of a group or committee.

You will learn how to really listen to what the other person is saying so you fully understand the message. You will learn how your body language enhances or depreciates your message, and how to interpret the body language of your listeners.

You will also learn how to make your written communications—whether they are letters, memos, emails or text messages—clear, concise, complete and more appealing to the readers.

To get the most out of this book, read all of it first to absorb the overall concept of giving and getting ideas and information. Then reread each chapter and start applying the guidelines for achieving each of the areas covered. This will start you on the track to be a better communicator—a major step forward on the road to success.

Arthur R. Pell, Ph.D.
Editor

1

....

GETTING IDEAS ACROSS TO OTHERS

Don M. was furious. "I explained in detail how to do that job. He told me he understood and now has messed it all up. It has to be done all over again."

How often has this happened to you? You give detailed instructions to a subordinate, explain a concept to an associate, describe a procedure to a customer—leave feeling that it is clearly understood and later find out it was not understood at all. Many problems could be avoided and much time saved if we could only be assured that what we communicate is received by the other party in the way we expected it to.

Is the Message Really Understood?

When Don gave his subordinate detailed instructions, what question do you think he asked when he completed his statement? You guessed right. He asked, "Did you understand?"

1

What do you think the subordinate answered? Again you're right. He surely said, "Yes, I do." Just because somebody says he or she understands does not mean he or she really does. Some people only think they understood what has been said and of course, they respond that they do understand. However, because their interpretation may be different from that of the person giving the information, there was no real understanding at all.

Other people understand only a part of what has been communicated yet assume they understand all of it. Still others do not understand it at all but are too embarrassed to tell their boss that they do not understand, so they say they do and try to figure it out for themselves. In these situations, no real communication has been accomplished and it is likely that errors will be made, misconceptions will develop; time will be wasted, tempers lost, and work will not be accomplished.

How do good communicators get their ideas across? Let's look at some of the responses to a survey made concerning office managers, factory supervisors, sales managers, and other administrative executives.

Betty M. office manager of a travel agency in New York City, reported that she never asks the employee if he or she understands the instructions. Instead, she asks the subordinate to tell her what he or she is going to do. "I give them a quiz," Betty told us. "If I give a clerk a project to complete, after I explain it, I ask her just what she is going to do. In case there is a different interpretation from what I had in mind, we can correct it on the spot before it becomes a problem. If the project is a complex one, I ask a variety of questions such as: 'What will you do if X happens?' and 'Suppose Y develops?'"

Among Betty's responsibility is teaching the clerical staff how to operate the computers used in making reservations and purchasing, and issuing airline tickets. She commented, "To be sure that I can depend on the clerk to operate that computer correctly, in addition to asking them questions, I have them show me on the computer just how they will handle a variety of problems. By having them actually work on the computer, I can see for myself how much they have learned and mastered."

Is the Message Accepted?

Understanding what is communicated is a basic criterion for good communication, but there is another factor which is equally important. What is communicated must not only be understood, the other party must accept it. The manager tells a clerk that an assignment must be completed by 3 o'clock in the afternoon. There is no doubt that the clerk knows exactly what the manager meant, but she says to herself, "no way." Do you think the job will be completed by 3? Not likely. Unless the person doing the job feels it is reasonable and attainable, he or she will not put forth the efforts to meet that time limit.

Louise R., who owns and manages a building maintenance service in Rock Hill, South Carolina, handles situations like this by soliciting the participation of her workers. Usually there is a team of men and woman involved in the project. She brings them together and first tells them what is required and the reason for the deadline. She then asks them when they think it can be done and what other suggestions they may have. Often they come up with solutions that are even better than what might have been determined solely by management.

From time to time, Louise learns from these meetings that overtime or extra help is needed and that her original estimate of time was overly optimistic. Because her people know she encourages their participation and listens to them, she gets more cooperation from them in tough situations when extra effort, energy and commitment are needed.

Plan What to Say

Whether we're addressing a group or having a one-to-one conversation, we should think out our message and how we plan to present it in advance. Sometimes we'll have to think on our feet with little or no time to prepare, but more often than not, when required to discuss something, we can prepare even on a short notice.

Know the Subject

On the job, we'll usually communicate with others about subjects we're thoroughly familiar with: the work we're doing, matters in our own area of expertize, or company-related problems. Still, we should review the facts to be sure that we have a hold on all the available information and are prepared to answer any questions.

From time to time, we may be asked to report on matters with which we are unfamiliar. Our company may want to purchase a new type of computer software, for example, and ask us to check it out.

> Learn as much as possible about the subject. Know ten times more than needed for the presentation.
> Prepare notes about the advantages and disadvantages of the proposed purchase, solution, and so on.

› Whether you are to make this report to one person (the boss, for example) or to a group of managers or technical specialists, be prepared to answer questions about any subject that might come up.

Know the Audience

Even the most skilled communicators fail to get their message across if the audience can't understand them. Half of good communication is understanding your audience. Choose words that your listeners can easily comprehend. If the people you are addressing come from a technical background, use technical terminology to communicate; the listeners would clearly and readily understand these special terms. But if you are to talk about a technical subject matter to an audience unfamiliar with it, drop the technical language. If your listeners can't understand your vocabulary, the message would be lost.

For example, Charles, an engineer whose work primarily involves dealing with other engineers is accustomed to using technical terms all the time. Now let's say he's called on to make a presentation to the company's finance department to arrange the funding for a new engineering project. It's Charles's responsibility, not the audience's, to ensure that the message gets across. If he can explain the technical matter in layperson's terms, he should do so. However, if it's necessary to use technical language, Charles must take the time to explain a term the first time he uses it, and at least once again if he feels that it needs reinforcement.

Those convinced against their will
are of the same opinion still.

Dale Carnegie

Speaking Clearly

We've all heard speakers who mumble, speak too fast or too slowly or have difficult-to-understand accents. If one does not articulate clearly, much of the message he or she is attempting to communicate would be lost to the listeners. Poor articulation is relatively easy to improve. Some ways to accomplish this will be discussed in Chapter 4.

Body Language

Some of the behaviors we exhibit without realizing it, can have an enormous impact on how we make an impression. Studies by social linguists regarding face-to-face communication determined that only seven percent of the message transferred from one person to the other was expressed in the words spoken. About 38 percent of the meanings were transmitted through vocal characteristics—tone of the voice, pauses, emphasis, etc.—and an astonishing 55 percent of the total message was communicated through visual signals we classify as "body language." Often we are not aware of how this affects the way we are perceived by others.

Posture

Good (or bad) posture can be seen even from a distance and registers instantly in the viewer's emotional brain. It is less subtle than other nonverbal gestures because it involves our entire body.

In research projects, participants assume that subjects with excellent posture were more popular, ambitious, confidant, friendly, and intelligent than those with a more relaxed stance.

Expect that improved posture will feel awkward and exaggerated at first. Work on standing straight, square-shouldered, and balanced lower body.

Of all facial expressions, the smile is the most influential. Smiling can actually cause others to be more receptive to our point of view. When we smile, the other person nearly always smiles back. More than just a mirroring, it reflects the sudden surge of warmth and well-being.

An insincere smile is more damaging than no smile. Don't try to smile warmly with just the jaw muscles. A believable smile uses the entire face and happens spontaneously when we process a positive thought about the exchange in which we are engaged.

> *When you smile at other people, you are telling them in a subtle way that you like them, at least to some degree. They will get that meaning and will like you better. Try the smiling habit. You have nothing to lose.*
>
> *Dale Carnegie*

Eye Contact

When we look at our listener, it implies confidence, honesty, and interest in that person. Lack of eye contact is usually interpreted as a sign of fear, dishonesty, hostility, or boredom.

Research shows that in job interviews, candidates give more complete and revealing answers when the interviewer maintains eye contact. In classes, student's comprehension and retention of materials are directly related to the instructor's eye contact. On the other hand, do not stare into the other person's eyes. Look at his or her entire face.

How to understand the body language of our listeners will be discussed in chapter 3.

Televise the Messages

We receive information from all five senses. Ideas and impressions develop from smelling, tasting and feeling, but most of the data that our mind processes come from hearing and seeing—audio and video. This has been significantly changed in this era of television. Television has merged audio and video so that those of us who have been brought up watching this medium from "Sesame Street" to today's news are accustomed to receiving information simultaneously through our eyes and ears. By applying this "simulcast" approach to our communication with other people, our messages will come across more effectively.

Don't Just Tell—Show!

In training her people to handle insurance claims, Joan found that when she drew a flow chart while describing the process, it was much more easily understood. As she taught each phase, she outlined them by drawing boxes around each step, as well as drew arrows showing the movement from step-to-step.

Steve learned, from failed experience, that telling his people how to do the job was not enough. Unless he took his trainees from place to place in the warehouse, they had difficulty in understanding what he was teaching. This was a very time consuming effort. He simplified the training by designing a model of the storerooms with which he could orient his people as he told them about the work they would be doing.

Many executives have flip charts or chalkboards in their offices so that they can use visual means to enhance their oral communications. By illustrating the subjects with charts, graphs, diagrams or sketches, what is being presented becomes far more effective. When there is a subject in which the listening is augmented by visual images, people tend to learn it faster and remember it longer.

One of the most popular professors at Syracuse University's School of Journalism was also a cartoonist. He drew cartoons and caricatures as he lectured. His colleagues scoffed at this and considered it very unprofessional. "He's just amusing his students—not teaching," they claimed. Yes, his students did find it amusing, but they absorbed a great deal more information than they would from just plain lecturing, and years later could still recall his teachings.

How to use visual aids effectively will be discussed in chapter 5.

> *Your purpose is to make your listeners see what you saw, hear what you heard, feel what you felt. Relevant detail, couched in concrete, colorful language, is the best way to recreate the incident as it happened and to picture it for the listeners.*
>
> *Dale Carnegie*

Creating Visual Images on the Telephone

The one media in which we still cannot use visual augmentation is the telephone. Yet, we can help our listeners "see" what we are saying by drawing word pictures. A word picture enables the listener to picture in the mind's eye what we are saying.

When we are asked for directions to our building, we say: "Take I-95 to Exit 23, that's Mulberry Street. Make a right off the ramp and drive to the fourth traffic light, that's 17th Avenue. Make a left on 17th Avenue and drive twelve blocks to Smith Road. Make a right on Smith Road and drive five blocks. We are number 2345 Smith Road."

That's clear. But now let's give these directions using word pictures: "Take I-95 to Exit 23, that's Mulberry Street. Make a right off the ramp and drive to the fourth traffic light. There's a Texaco station on your left and a McDonald's on the right. That's 17th Ave. Make a left on 17th Ave. Drive to the firehouse, that's Smith Road. Make a right and drive towards the yellow brick building on the left. That's our office, 2345 Smith Road."

Isn't that easier? The visitor does not have to count lights or blocks or look for street names. He or she can just seek out landmarks that have been visually presented.

Televise the Future

Successful sales people use word pictures. Audrey sells computers; in discussing the problems faced by one of her prospects, she learned that he was primarily concerned with the messy office that he supervised. "Papers and files are all over the place," he complained. "And I can never find the files that I need—they're always out, probably, in one of those piles."

After describing the technical aspects of her company's product, she said: "Let's look ahead to six months from now. You walk into the office. There are no piles of paper on desks and chairs. Your people are all working at their computers. You need a file; you sit down at a terminal and key in the file name. Instantly, the information desired appears on your screen. No waiting, No frustration."

Audrey has drawn a word picture of the future. The

manager does not require much imagination to visualize this and recognize the value of making the purchase.

Barriers to Clear Communication

No matter how good the preparation and presentation of our messages, often what is received is not exactly what has been sent. Barriers have cropped up, which impede the communication.

Some of these major barriers are psychological, not physical. We may have perfect articulation and choose our words wisely, but the static develops in intangible areas: assumptions, attitudes, and the emotional baggage each of us has.

Check Out Assumptions

We have a pretty good idea about what causes a particular problem and how to solve it. In discussing it with others, we assume that they know as much about it as we do, so what we say is based on the assumption that they have know-how even though they don't. As a result, we don't give them adequate information.

Be Aware of Our Attitude

Another barrier to communication is the attitudes of the sender and the receiver. A manager who is arrogant will convey his feelings in the way directions and informations are given. He or she may appear to be talking down to staff members. This causes resentment, which blocks communication. In order for the message to be received, it must not only be understood but also accepted by the receiver. When resentment develops, acceptance is unlikely.

An employee who is busy resenting the leader's attitude does not really "hear" what's being said. Good leaders avoid such indicators of arrogance as sarcasm and "pulling rank" when dealing with staff members.

Watch for Preconceptions

People tend to hear what they expect to hear. The message they receive is distorted by any information they have already heard about the subject. So if the new information is different from what's expected, they might reject it as being incorrect. Rather than actually hearing the new message, they may be hearing what their minds are telling them.

What does this mean? People must be trained to keep their minds open. When someone tells them something, they must make an extra effort to listen and to evaluate the new information objectively, instead of blocking it out because it differs from their preconceptions.

In communicating with others, try to learn their preconceptions. If they are people we work with regularly, we probably know how they view most of the matters we discuss. When presenting your views to them, take into consideration what they already believe. If their beliefs differ from yours, be prepared to make the effort to jump over those hurdles.

Prejudices and Biases—Ours and Theirs

Our biases for or against a person influence the way we receive their messages. We listen more attentively and are more likely to accept ideas from somebody we like and respect. Contrarily, we tend to blot out inputs from people we don't like, and reject their ideas.

Perception is reality in the mind of the perceiver. Unless our perception of a situation and of those with whom we are communicating are congruent, we would be working at cross-purposes.

Biases also affect the way subject matter is received. People turn a deaf ear to opposing viewpoints concerning matters about which they have strong feelings. Carol is a good example of such a person. As company controller, she is fixated on reducing costs. She won't even listen to any discussion that might increase costs no matter what the long-term benefits may be. To sell her on an original idea, we have to convince her how although there may be an immediate increase in costs, in the long run—it will be cost effective.

Many people are not even conscious of their own biases. Take the time to analyze why we have made certain decisions in the past. Have they been overly influenced by our biases? Follow these six steps:

1. Become aware of your biases.
2. Identify why you hold these biases.
3. Acknowledge shared characteristics.
4. Put your biases aside, and maintain an open mind.
5. Make an effort to consider other people's ideas objectively.
6. Don't allow a negative experience to revive your biases.

Be Aware of Our Emotional State

We've all had bad days. And on one of those bad days, one of our associates comes to us all excited about a new idea. How do we react? We probably think: "I have enough on my platter already, who needs this now?" Our mind is closed and the message doesn't come through. Not only must we be aware of our own emotional state when giving or receiving a message, we must also consider the emotional state of our subordinate.

An important project comes up and we go over to two of our staff members, Dan and Joan, to discuss it. Joan is enthusiastic about the job; Dan is skeptical. Why? Dan is annoyed because he is busy working on another project and he wants to concentrate on that. He feels we are inconsiderate to assign him another job.

Always test the temperature of the water before stepping into the tub. A brief conversation with Dan and Joan about their current activities would have brought out how much time Dan was spending on his current project. When presenting the new assignment, make the observation that what he is doing now is important, and you are happy with his progress. Show that the reason you chose him for the new assignment is because it will complement his current work.

Channels: The Distortion Between Sender and Receiver

In communication, a major source of interference and distortion is the path the message takes from sender to receiver. In many large organizations, communications must flow through set channels. The more extensive the channels, the more likely that distortion will occur. This can be illustrated in the popular party game where one person whispers an incident to his or her neighbor, who repeats it to the next person, and this continues around the room. By the time it is retold to the originator, the story is completely different.

It is not unusual for a piece of information passed orally "through channels" to be distorted at each station, so that what the receiver receives is not at all what the sender sent.

One way to alleviate this difficulty is to use written mode of communication. Writing is more difficult to distort, though interpretation of what is written may vary from station to station. Even so, writing has certain disadvantages: Many matters can't or shouldn't be communicated in writing. Writing is time consuming. For urgent matters and matters of transient interest, writing is not appropriate.

A more effective way is to shorten channels and allow for bypassing where feasible. The fewer stations along the way, the less chance for distortion. The main reason for using channels is to ensure that people who are responsible for a project are kept aware of everything that applies to it. This makes sense, but it is often overdone. If a matter involves policy decisions or major areas of activity, channels are important. But a great portion of the communication in companies concerns routine matters. Using channels for these may not only distort the message but could also slow down the work.

Be Open to Feedback

Perhaps the most challenging aspect of managing our external image is the difficulty in seeing ourselves as others see us. Research indicates that we are probably more critical of ourselves than others are of us. At the same time, we may be unaware of some of our own negative traits that need to be corrected.

These are some ways to gain an accurate view of our own external image:

> Viewing and listening to videotapes of ourself speaking at meetings.
> Rehearsing our talks in front of a mirror.

> Getting honest critiques from trusted associates.

> Carefully monitoring audience reactions.

It's a good idea to have a "coach" help identify and work with you to overcome communication problems. Help in this field is available in most communities by professional speech coaches or hands-on seminars like the Dale Carnegie's "High Impact Presentations" program.

Assigning Work

One of the most important communication functions of a manager or supervisor is assigning work to his or her staff. Often we hear the complaint: "I don't understand why my people can't follow orders. I give them clear instructions and still they get it all wrong."

How often have we made comments like that or heard other supervisors lament their people's inability to get things done right. Perhaps, the cause is not that our people are inept, but that we are not assigning work as effectively as it should be done.

Planning the Assignment

As pointed out at the beginning of this chapter, our message must be planned. Too often supervisors do not take the time to prepare assignments. They know what has to be done and assume that all that is necessary is to order a subordinate to do it, and it will be done.

Planning starts with having a clear concept of what must be accomplished. Even if we have done this type of work many times, it is important to think it through once again.

Think how the subordinate views this. If you had never seen this project before, what would you want to know? List the objectives you wish to attain, the information needed to attain it, the materials, tools, support sources and whatever else is needed to do the work.

A very important part of the planning is to determine who will be given the assignment. In selecting these people bear in mind the importance of the assignment. If it is one in which it is essential that the work be done immediately and with little supervision, choose people who have demonstrated competence in the past, in this type of work. However, if it is an area where there is adequate time for you to provide guidance, it may be advantageous to assign it to less skilled people, and use this project as a means of training and development of their skills.

Communicating the Assignment

Barbara was frustrated. She had given Carol a detailed description of what she wanted to be done and Carol had assured her she understood. Now, a week later, Carol turned in work that was all wrong. Her excuse: "I thought that's what you wanted."

Norman was upset. His boss had just given him a deadline that he felt was totally unrealistic. "He's out of line," Norman thought, "There's no way I can do this much work in such a short time. I'll do what I can, but I know I'm not going to make it."

As pointed out earlier in this chapter, the supervisor must assure himself or herself that the subordinate fully understands and accepts the instruction.

Get a Plan of Action

On assignments that will take any significant amount of time, ask the subordinate to prepare a plan of action before starting the job. This should—just what is to be done, when it is scheduled to be done, and what support may be needed.

Rita's assignment was to arrange travel plans for 20 salespeople from all over the country, to attend a meeting in Chicago. Before starting the assignment, she wrote a plan of action in which she covered every aspect of the assignment including notifying the salespeople, making airline and hotel reservations, and assuring that all the participants received their tickets within adequate time. The plan included timetables for starting and completing each phase and indication of what assistance she would need for the same. Going over this with her boss, she was able to iron out any misunderstandings or potential problems before starting.

Note that Rita put her plan of action into writing. By doing this, both she and her boss were able to check any time how the plan was proceeding and catch the problems-if any-early.

Follow-up

No matter how well any assignment is planned, it is incumbent upon a supervisor to follow-up from time to time to assure it is going according to the plan.

Alan believes that if he follows up too frequently, his people will feel that he doesn't trust them. "I want my people to be true participants. Once I agree to their plan of action, I must assume they will follow it. If I check them, I defeat what I am trying to project."

Alan has a point, but he still has the ultimate responsibility for the success of his department; the assignments are not properly completed, it would reflect on his ability. To assure that assignments are accomplished, follow-up is necessary. However, it can be achieved without causing the people to feel we don't trust them.

The key to Alan's philosophy of management is participation. Therefore, follow-up should be done in a participatory manner. Instead of Alan looking over his people's shoulders or surprising them with unexpected check-ups, the follow-ups should be built into the plan of action. When the subordinate develops the plan, checkpoints should be incorporated throughout the project. After certain phases of the project have been completed, the subordinate would meet Alan and go over what has been done. He or she should be encouraged to critique the work and perhaps suggest new or additional matters that might be incorporated in the assignment. Of course, Alan would make appropriate comments and suggestions as well. In this way the follow-up becomes part of the participative approach as well as acts as a stimulus to the subordinate to achieve even greater success in meeting the challenges of the assignment.

Cultivating Diplomacy and Tact

The way in which we communicate can elicit positive or negative emotions. If we communicate aggressively, without respect or sensitivity, defensive and angry emotions can prevent others from hearing the message we are trying to convey. Communicating with diplomacy and tact is an approach that combines strength and sensitivity and keep emotions at bay. When we communicate with diplomacy and tact, we adapt our style to the person we are speaking to in order to put them at ease.

Most people tend to follow an individual style of communication. Research on communication styles have commonly placed people into one of the four categories:

> *Friendly style:* These people are casual, amiable, relationship focused, helpful, and warm. They do not like to argue and they look for positive feedbacks.

> *Analytical style:* These people are formal, methodical, and systematic. They are impressed with data and details. They look carefully at evidences, and use them to find answers and solutions to the problems discussed.

> *Excitable style:* These men and women are demonstrative and expressive.
They are prone to use gestures in making their points. They are more concerned with the big picture than the details— their main concern is what's in it for them.

> *Pragmatic style:* These people are goal oriented and focused on the objectives to be achieved. Even if they have strong opinions and viewpoints, they are willing to consider other options when presented with them.

> *Diplomatic and tactful style:* These people establish rapport based on the style with which the other person communicates.

Earn the Trust of the People

To be a good communicator, we must gain the trust and respect of the people with whom we are relating. To earn this:

1. Take others' interests to heart; ask questions, learn what

motivates them, and help them to learn and grow.

2. Listen sincerely with ears, eyes, and heart and without prejudice and judgment.

3. Honor and find merit in differences of opinion, biases, and diversity.

4. Involve others in decisions, display an open and accepting attitude, and be receptive to new ideas.

5. Be willing to negotiate and compromise, and be a mediator between others who have different points of view.

6. Think before speaking. Consider the audience, relationship, and environment when choosing your words and actions.

7. Use inclusive language, and communicate with diplomacy, tact, and sensitivity.

8. Speak confidently, decisively, and with authority; and offer evidence when stating opinions.

9. Stand up for your beliefs and non-negotiable values.

10. Be a modest expert and be willing to defer to another's expertize.

11. Be reliable: keep confidences, fulfill promises, and keep commitments.

12. Refrain from mood swings. Act consistently, rationally, fairly, honestly, and ethically.

13. Be a stellar role model act professionally and always walk the talk.

14. Demonstrate trust in others reveal your own thoughts and feelings frankly and openly.

15. Be authentic—demonstrate congruency between your words and actions.

16. Be approachable and available as a resource.

17. Be realistic when communicating goals and outcomes.
18. Accept responsibility and admit mistakes, downfalls, and disadvantages.
19. Deal directly with others. Do not partake in gossip and never talk behind someone's back.
20. Share the glory—give others credit for accomplishments.

Sum and Substance

> Whether you are presenting your ideas to a group or to just one person, prepare what you're going to say before you say it.

> Speak clearly and distinctly so that you could be easily understood. Speak with enthusiasm so that your audience doesn't fall asleep.

> Be aware of your body language

> Be prepared to overcome barriers that distort your communication.

> Know and control your biases.

> In assigning work, plan what you would say, communicate it clearly to the assignees, get feedback on whether what you said was received; follow-up to assure that it is accomplished.

> Assure that what you have communicated is not only understood but also accepted by the other party.

> Be tactful and diplomatic in all of your dealings with others.

2

....

THE ART OF GOOD
CONVERSATION

The ability to engage in interesting conversations is one of the greatest personal assets a man or woman can have. It is a great aid to business and social success and also makes for greater enjoyment of the company of other people.

There is nothing that enables us to make so good an impression, especially upon those who do not know us thoroughly, than the ability to converse well. To be a good conversationalist, to be able to interest people, to rivet their attention, to draw them to us naturally, by the very superiority of our conversational ability, is to be the possessor of a very great accomplishment. It not only helps to make a good impression upon strangers, it also helps us to make and keep friends. It opens doors and softens hearts. It makes us interesting in all sorts of company. It helps us to get on in the world. It sends you clients, patients, or customers. It is the tool that would enable you to persuade people to accept your ideas, follow your leadership, and buy your products.

People who can talk well, who have the art of putting things in an attractive way, who can interest others immediately by their power of speech, have an advantage over those who may know more than they do about the subject, but who cannot express themselves with ease or eloquence.

Conversation is a tremendous power developer. However, talking without thinking, without an effort to express oneself with clarity and conciseness would work against you. Mere chattering, or gossiping is not impressive. It lies too deep for such superficial effort. Nothing else will indicate our fineness or coarseness of culture, our breeding or lack of it, as quickly as our conversation. It tells our whole life's story. What we say, and how we say it, will betray all our secrets, will give the world our true measure.

What Makes a Good Conversationalist?

Intellect, brainpower, expertize in a field can be helpful, but it is not the main reason through which a good conversationalist holds the attention of others.

We must make people feel our empathy, and that they have met a sincere person. Don't greet people with a stiff "How do you do?" or "Glad to meet you," without feeling any sentiment. Be accommodative and adapt to different dispositions. Look people you meet squarely in the eye and make them aware of your personality. Greet them with a smile and kind words, that would make them want to meet you again.

Be Cordial

To be an accepted conversationalist, we must cultivate cordiality. We must fling the door of our heart wide open, and not, as many do, just leave it slightly ajar to indicate to the ones we meet: "You may peep in a bit, but you cannot come in until I know whether you will be a desirable acquaintance." A great many people are stingy of their cordiality. They seem to reserve it for some special occasion or for intimate friends. They think it is too precious to give out to everybody.

Do not be afraid to open our heart; fling the door wide open. Get rid of all reservations; do not meet a person as though you were afraid of making a mistake and doing what you would be glad to recall.

A warm, glad handshake and cordial greeting will create a bond of good-will between you and the people you meet. They will say to themselves: "Well, there is a really interesting personality. I want to know more about this man or woman. They see something in me, evidently, which most people do not see."

Cultivate the habit of being cordial, of meeting people with a warm, sincere greeting, and an open heart; it will do wonders for you. You would find the stiffness, diffidence and indifference, the cold lack of interest in everybody, which now so troubles you disappearing. People will see that you really take an interest in them, that you really want to know and please them. The practice of cordiality will revolutionize your social power. You would develop attractive qualities that you never before dreamed of possessing.

It's Not Just What We Say, but How We Say It

Keep in mind that we express ourselves not only through the words we utter, but also by the tone of the voice, the expression of the face, our gestures, and our bearing.

When Charles W. Eliot was president of Harvard, he said: "I recognize but one mental acquisition as an essential part of the education of a lady or gentleman the accurate and refined use of the mother tongue."

There is no accomplishment, no attainment that we can use so constantly and effectively, which will help us make and keep friends, as fine as a conversation. There is no doubt that the gift of language was intended to be a much greater accomplishment than the majority of us have ever made of it.

Cultivate Conversational Skills

Most of us are bunglers in our conversations because we do not make an art of it. We do not take the trouble or pains to learn to talk well. We do not read enough or think enough. Most of us express ourselves in sloppy language because it is so much easier to do so than it is to think before we speak, to make an effort to express ourselves with elegance, ease, and power.

Poor conversationalists excuse themselves for not trying to improve by saying, "good talkers are born, not made." We might as well say that good lawyers, good physicians, or good merchants are born, not made. All the success that good doctors or merchants or scientists or teachers, indeed the elite of any career enjoy is a direct result of hard work. This is the price of all achievement that is of value.

Many people owe their advancement largely to their ability to converse well. The ability to interest people in conversation, and to hold them, is a great power. People who have a bungling expression, who know something, but can never put it in logical, interesting, or commanding language, are always placed at a great disadvantage.

It is a great treat to listen to people who have cultivated the art of conversation. Their language flows with such liquid, limpid beauty; their words are chosen with such exquisite delicacy; taste, and accuracy, there is such a refinement in their diction that they charm everyone who hears them speak.

We may think we are poor and have no opportunity in life. We may be situated so that others are dependent upon us, and we may not be able to go to school or college, or to study music or art, as we long to do. We may be tied down to a depressing environment or tortured with an unsatisfied, disappointed objectives. None of these should prevent us from becoming an interesting talker, because in every sentence that we utter, we can practice the best form of expression. Every book we read, every person with whom we converse, who uses good speech can help us.

Few people think excessively about how they are going to express themselves. They use the first words that come to them. They do not think of forming a sentence so that it will have beauty, brevity, transparency, and power. The words flow from their lips helter-skelter, with little thought, arrangement or order.

Good reading, however, will not only broaden the mind and introduce new ideas, but it will also increase one's vocabulary, which is a great aid to conversations. Many people have good thoughts and ideas, but they cannot express them because of the poverty of their vocabulary. Yet some people do not have the right words to clothe their ideas and make them attractive. They repeatedly talk around in circles, because when they want a particular word to convey their exact meaning, they cannot find it.

If we are determined to talk well, we must associate with educated, cultured people. If we seclude ourselves, though we may be a college graduates, we will be a poor conversationalist.

We all sympathize with people, especially the timid and shy, who have that awful feeling of repression and stifling of thought, when they make an effort to say something and cannot. Timid young people often suffer keenly in this area when attempting to express their thoughts at their schools or colleges. But even great orators have gone through similar experience when they first attempted to speak in public, and were often deeply humiliated by blunders and failures. There is no other way, however, to become a good conversationalist than by constantly trying to express oneself efficiently and elegantly.

If we find that our ideas fly from us when we attempt to express them, that we stammer and flounder about for words which we are unable to find, we may be sure that every honest effort we make, even if we fail in our attempt, will make it all the way easier for us to speak well the next time. It is remarkable, if we keep on trying, how quickly we can conquer our awkwardness and self-consciousness, and gain ease of manner and convenience of expression.

All good conversationalists have felt a power come to them from the listener that they never felt before, which often stimulates and inspires them to take up fresh endeavors. The mingling of thought with thought, the contact of mind with mind, develops new powers, as the mixing of two chemicals often produces a new third substance.

You can make more friends in two months by becoming interested in other people than you can in two years by trying to get other people interested in you.

Dale Carnegie

Be Truly Interested in Others

Many of us are not only poor conversationalists, but we are poor listeners as well. We are too impatient to listen. Instead of being attentive and eager to drink in the story or the information, we do not have enough respect for the talker to keep quiet. We look around impatiently, perhaps play out a pattern with our fingers on a chair or a table, hitch about as if we were bored and anxious to get away, and thereby, interrupt speakers before they reach a conclusion. In fact, we are such impatient people that we have no time for anything except pushing ahead, elbowing our way through the crowd to get the position or the money desired.

Impatience is a conspicuous characteristic of many of us. Everything bores us which does not bring more business, or more money, or which does not help to attain the positions for which we are striving.

Instead of enjoying our friendships, we inclined to look upon our friends as so rungs in a ladder, and to value them terms of the number of patients, clients, customers they send, or their ability to give a boost to our political position.

One cause for our conversational decline is a lack of empathy. We are too selfish, too engaged in our own welfare, and wrapped up in our own little world, and too intent upon our own self-promotion to be interested in others. No one can be a good conversationalist unless they are empathetic. We must be able to enter into another's life, to live it with the other person, in order to be a good listener or a good talker.

If we make ourselves empathetic we would be able to enter into the life of the people with whom we are conversing, and touch them along the lines of their interests. No matter how much we may know about a subject, if it does not happen to interest those with whom we are talking, our efforts would be largely lost.

It is sad sometimes, to see people standing around at the average reception or club gathering, dumb, almost helpless, and powerless to enter heartily into the conversation because they are too self-absorbed. They do not enter heartily into the lives of others, or abandon themselves to the occasion enough to become good talkers.

They are cold, reserved and distant because their minds are somewhere else, their affections on their own affairs. There are only two things that interest them: business and their own little world. If we talk about these things, they are interested at once; but they do not care about our affairs, how we get on, what our ambition is, or how they can help us. Their conversations will never reach a high standard while they live in such a feverish, selfish, and unempathetic state.

Be Tactful

Great conversationalists are always very tactful—interesting without offending. Some people have the peculiar quality of touching the best that is in us; others stir up the bad. Every time they come in contact they irritate us. Others are joyous and agreeable; they never inflame our sensitive spots. They radiate all that is spontaneous and sweet and beautiful.

Lincoln was a master of the art of making himself interesting to everybody he met. He put people at ease with his stories and jokes, and made them feel so completely at home in his presence that they opened up their mental treasures to him without reserve. Strangers were always glad to talk to him because he was so cordial and quaint, and always gave more than he got.

A sense of humor such as Lincoln's is of course a great addition to one's conversational power. Yet not everyone can be funny; and if we lack sense of humor, we only make ourselves ludicrous by attempting to be funny.

Good conversationalists, however, are not overly serious. They don't overwhelm us with miniscule details. Facts, statistics can be weary, so they supplement them with illustrations and anecdotes to make their points. Vivacity is absolutely necessary. Heavy conversations can be boring. But caution: if it is too light, although it may be amusing, it may not help achieve your objective.

Therefore, to be a good conversationalist we must be spontaneous, buoyant, natural, empathetic, and must show a spirit of good will. We must feel a spirit of helpfulness, and must enter heart and soul into things that interest others. We must get the attention of people and hold it by interesting them, and we can only interest them by a warm empathy—a real friendly empathetic attitude. If we are cold, distant, and unempathetic we cannot hold someone's attention.

Be open-minded and tolerant. People who violate a sense of taste, of justice, and of fairness, never interest others. They tightly lock all the approaches to their inner selves and the conversation is perfunctory, mechanical and without life or feeling.

To be a success anywhere, develop the power to express yourself in strong, effective, and interesting language. It is not necessary to give a stranger an inventory of your possessions in order to show that you have achieved something.

Our attitude, the spirit we radiate, our personality, will have everything to do with our conversational proficiency. The impression we make will be a tremendous factor in our success. Only then we would carry the conviction and give the impression of mastership, and that is half the battle won.

Learn and Remember Names

Remember, a person's name is, to that person, the sweetest and most important sound in any language.

Dale Carnegie

When meeting a new person, make a special effort to learn his or her name. Often names may be mumbled during an introduction, especially when more than one person is being introduced at the same time. If it is not clear, it is not impolite to ask for it be repeated. Using the name during the conversation helps set it firmly in our mind.

Follow these suggestions:

> Determine which part of the name to use. Americans usually use first names, unless the other person is significantly older or has higher authority, then use Mr./Ms. until he or she says, "First name, please." In other cultures, one always uses the formal 'Mr.', 'Mrs.' 'Ms.' or a title, 'Dr.', 'Professor', etc. unless invited to be less formal.

> Create a mind picture, linking the name with the person. Don't think in words—think in pictures. When we meet Julie, picture her bedecked with *jewelry*; Sandy reminds us of a beach, and George is visualized as standing at the edge of a *gorge*.

> Repeat the names immediately in your conversation, but don't overdo or it would look phony. Do it about once in three to four minutes of conversation, and when you leave.

> If the name is same as or similar to that of a relative, friend, or another person you know, picture the new person with that person.

> Most important, use it, use it, use it until it is firmly established in your mind.

Learn About the Other Person

When we meet a new person, it is important to get as much information about that person as possible. One way to obtain this is asking questions. However, this should not be an interrogation. Just a few well-chosen questions would get the ball rolling and the conversation would flow.

This is a delicate process, as we do not want to appear to be nosy. Ask only those questions which are appropriate for the situation in which you are involved. For example, some questions are appropriate when talking to a person on a business matter; others in social situations, etc.

In a social situation questions about the area in which one lives, hobbies or interests, family or mutual acquaintances are often good starters. Other good conversation openers are about schools or colleges they have attended, recent current events they participated in, or a comment made by the other person.

When meeting people in a business setting, good starters are questions about the industry and company the person represents, news items that affect that industry, questions about the nature of his or her job or career.

It's not necessary to have a list of questions we plan to ask. Once the conversation is underway, comments and responses would flow easily.

Conversational Styles

The manner in which we communicate with others, whether it is in a one-to-one conversation or when speaking to a group can influence how others perceive us. We may come across as passive, aggressive, or assertive.

Some of the traits manifested by passive people are:

> They are more concerned about others, often to their own personal detriment.
> They are often stressed internally, although it may not be obvious to others.
> They are likely to have low self-esteem.
> They are more concerned with being liked than being respected.

- They build others up even at their own expense.
- They take blame rather than blame others.
- They avoid confrontation.
- When action is needed, they ask for it indirectly in the form of a suggestion or as a wish.

The opposite of the passive style is the aggressive approach. Aggressive people manifest the following characteristics:

- They are overly self-centered.
- They are often internally stressed.
- They lack self-esteem, but will not admit it even to themselves.
- They are usually not liked or respected by others.
- They put others down by sarcasm or derogatory remarks.
- They try to control everything and everyone.
- When errors or failures occur, they blame others and never consider themselves responsible.
- They enjoy and seek confrontation with people with opposing views.
- If in a powerful position, they force others to follow.
- They are often verbally abusive to opponents.
- When action is needed, they present it in the form of a demand or command.

Effective communicators take a middle course. They are confident and assertive.

- They stand up for their own rights, but are also sensitive to others with whom they are speaking.
- If stressed, they deal with it and then move on.
- They have a strong, positive self-image.
- They are direct and honest.

- They earn the respect of others.
- They show their appreciation of others.
- They own up to their own errors and failures and expect others to own up to theirs.
- They do not seek confrontation. If others disagree, they will work to persuade them in a non-threatening, objective discussion.
- They are always willing to listen to others.
- When action is needed, they state what should be done, and work with others to accomplish it.

It is not easy to change our personality, but if we want to be better communicators, if we identify our style as passive or aggressive, we must make an effort to achieve the assertive, confident approach.

Our Telephone Personality

Every time we pick up the telephone—whether to make or receive a call—we leave an impression on the person at the other end of the line. Often, the only image that the person will have of us and our company will be derived from this conversation.

In face-to-face communication, there are many tools that help us to make good (or bad) impressions: our facial expressions, our gestures, and our use of props or visual aids. With the telephone, there is only one tool: our voice. Most people do not really hear themselves as others hear them. The best way to obtain a true concept of how we sound to others is to record several telephone calls and evaluate how they come across when we replay them. Most important, of course, is how we sound. Listen to those recordings and make the necessary changes needed to improve its quality.

Check the Attitude

One of the prime characteristics of effective dealing with others is to be friendly. Do we sound friendly on those recordings or do we sound annoyed? This call might have come at an inopportune time. We could be pressed by a demanding boss, a deadline that we were trying to meet, or a crisis in the department, but the caller does not know (or care about) this. We must discipline ourselves to put everything other than that phone call out of our minds.

If you are upset about something, before picking up the phone, take a deep breath, relax your muscles and clear your mind. Be calm, be attentive and the impression you wish to make—a genuine interest in what that person is saying—will be projected.

Telephone Tactics When Receiving a Call

Answer the phone promptly. In an official situation, the phone should not ring more than three times before it is answered. If you are on another call; either use your voicemail or put the current call on hold, pick up the new call and either request them to wait for a few minutes, or take the number and call back. If you plan to be away from our desk for more than a few minutes, arrange for somebody to take the calls or set the voicemail to answer after three rings.

Always state who you are immediately. Instead of saying "hello," say "Engineering Dept., Sam Johnson speaking." We cannot assume that the person who is calling knows who we are. If we do not know the caller, ask for his or her name. If it is an unusual name, ask how it is spelled. Write it down. When responding, use the caller's name. It demonstrates our sincere interest in that person and his or her problem. If we cannot provide the answers to the caller's questions within a very few minutes, it would be better to advise that we would call back rather than putting them on hold for a long time. If he or she prefers to hold the call or it takes longer than anticipated to respond, get back to them frequently so that they know that they haven't been abandoned.

One of the most irritating aspects of telephoning a company is to be told that you will be transferred to another person and then be disconnected. If it is necessary to transfer a call, always tell the person to whom they are going to be transferred to and give the caller that person's extension or phone number (if different from yours). It is also a good idea to obtain the caller's number, so that if disconnected, we can call them back to respond, not only to their direct questions, but also to implied objections.

When Martha called the Mail Order Department to complain about receiving damaged merchandise, she seemed upset when she was told to return it by United Parcel Service. The customer service representative recognized her concern and quickly told Martha that she did not have to make a trip to the UPS shipping center, but that they would arrange for UPS to pick up the package at her home.

By anticipating her concern, not only did the customer service representative make the customer feel better about the situation, but made a friend for the company.

Telephone Tactics When Making a Call

The beginning and end of a telephonic conversation are critical points. Begin the call with a welcoming attitude that shows you are glad to be talking to that person, and recognize that the call is important to them. If you are not known to that person, tell them who you are and why you are calling.

"Good morning Mrs. Samuels, as a mother who has children in our schools, I know you are concerned about the quality of education in this district. This is Blanche H., campaign manager for Diane McGrath, who is running for the school board presidency."

After making the presentation, listening and responding to questions, conclude in a positive way. "Thank you for your attention. I look forward to seeing you at the board meeting next Tuesday."

Plan all calls before picking up the phone. If you have to cover several items in a call, make a list of these items. Note the major points you wish to make for each of them. Follow your plan when talking and the call would be accomplished more effectively and in less time.

Listen to the other person. His or her responses may make it necessary to adjust your original plan. Ask questions and pay close attention to the responses. This is true for all communications, but particularly valuable with phone calls because we do not have the advantage of watching the non-verbal signals visible in face-to-face dealings. Learn to "read" the nuances of changes in inflection and voice tone. Think about the message you plan to send from the listener's point of view.

Small Talk

There is nothing really small about "small talk." This non-business style of conversation has the potential to build connections and become the foundation for ongoing relationships.

Becoming adept at small talks doesn't require an exhaustive knowledge of current events. It simply requires the ability to make the other person focus on his/her favorite topic, by asking questions that indicate interest. Even talking about the weather can be an ice-breaker. This is a sure-fire way to build rapport.

Be a Better Listener

Asking questions that will elicit appropriate information is the first step in getting to know people, but no matter how well chosen the questions we ask, unless we carefully listen to the responses, we would only understand a fraction of information that is provided. Honing our listening skills are important in all conversations.

Some techniques to help us become a better listener will be discussed in the following chapter.

Conversation Effectiveness Checklist

Review some recent conversations—whether it was in person or on the telephone. Did you:

> Smile? Even on the telephone, a smile is reflected in your voice and your attitude.
> If appropriate, use small talk to break the ice?
> Remember and use the person's name?

- Make a connection with the other person by observing his or her traits, values, or achievements?
- Establish common ground?
- Show respect for the other person's time?
- Show sensitivity to issues of diversity and avoid controversial subjects?
- Demonstrate a sincere desire to learn about the person by asking thoughtful questions?
- Fully listen and focus on what the person was saying?
- Ask how you can help?
- Talk in terms of the other person's interests?
- Tell them something of interest that they might not already know?
- Give sincere praise or a genuine compliment with evidence?

Sum and Substance

Dos for Good Conversation

- Do be prepared. A good conversationalist engages his or her listeners in a stimulating conversation. Hone your conversational skills by keeping up with trends and current events.
- Do learn the name of the other person and use it in the conversation.
- Do make eye contact. Looking directly at the other person is a indication that you are listening. Don't stare at the other person. Yes, look at their eyes, but move our eyes around so you could observe their entire face.
- Do speak clearly and audibly. If you are frequently asked to

speak up or to repeat yourself, you're probably not speaking clearly. Record and listen to your conversations.

> Do seek professional help from a voice coach to overcome poor speaking habits.

> Do use language and images familiar to the listener. You get more out of a conversation with someone who speaks and thinks like you do, than someone who uses a different vocabulary.

> Do speak the conversational style of the person with whom you're talking to.

> Do use different words and inflection when speaking to business associates than when conversing with the teenager down the street.

> Do stick to the topic. Conversation stealers are people who jump in on our story to change the focus to themselves or to something that they know more about.

> Do know when to speak and when to listen. Conversation should be a matter of give and take. Each person involved in a conversation needs to speak and each needs to listen. Participate but don't monopolize.

> Do express an interest in what's being said. Acknowledge statements with a nod, comment or question when appropriate.

> Do ask open-ended questions to promote communication— that is, questions that require more than a yes or no response.

Don'ts for Good Conversation

> Don't speak too fast or too slow. We've all been in conversations with people who talk so fast that we can't keep up, or so slowly that by the time they finish expressing their thought, we've forgotten the topic.

- ➤ Don't mumble or swallow your words.
- ➤ Don't talk too softly or too loud. Adjust your volume by the closeness or distance from your listener(s).
- ➤ Don't monopolize the conversation. Give the other person(s) a chance to talk.
- ➤ Don't brag or boast. A conversation should be an interchange of ideas and thoughts—not an ego-trip.
- ➤ Don't interrogate. Questions should be presented in a friendly and non-aggressive manner. Use open-end questions so the other person can express his or her ideas freely.
- ➤ Don't interrupt. Let the other person complete his or her comment before presenting yours.
- ➤ Don't talk over another person. Talking while the other person is still speaking is not only impolite, but your may miss the point he or she is making.
- ➤ Don't close your mind to what is being said. Open-mindedness is essential if you want to understand another's point of view.

3

....

LISTEN! REALLY LISTEN!

o you really listen? Suppose one of your colleagues brings a problem to you and asks for help. You may begin by listening attentively, but before you know it, your mind wanders. Instead of listening to the problem, you're thinking about the pile of work on your desk, the telephone call you were planning to make when this colleague walked into your office, of the argument you had with your daughter when you drove her to school this morning. You hear your colleague's words, but you're not really listening.

This happens to all of us. Why? Our minds can process ideas considerably faster than we can talk. When someone is talking to us, our mind tends to race ahead and we complete the speaker's sentence in our mind—sometimes correctly, but often differently from what the speaker says. You hear what your mind dictates, but not what is eventually said.

This is human nature. But that is not an excuse for being a bad listener. Take the following test to determine how good a listener you are.

Evaluate Your Listening Skills

Answer 'yes' or 'no' to the following questions:

- Do you keep interrupting when somebody is trying to tell you something?
- Do you look at papers during the discussion?
- Do you come to the conclusion even before you hear the whole story?
- Does your body language signal lack of interest?
- Do you hear only what you want to hear and block out everything else?
- Do you show impatience with speakers?
- Do you spend more time talking than listening?
- Does your mind wander during the discussion?
- Do you think about your rebuttal or responses while the other person is still speaking?
- Do you ignore nonverbal signals from the speaker that might indicate that the speaker wants you to respond?

If you answered 'yes' to any of these questions, you should concentrate on improving your listening skills.

Becoming an Active Listener

An active listener not only pays close attention to what the other party is saying but also asks questions, makes comments, and reacts verbally and nonverbally to what is being said.

One way of improving your listening skill is to play an

active role. Instead of just sitting or standing with your ears open, follow these guidelines:

➤ Look at the speaker. Eye contact is one way of showing interest, but don't overdo it. Look at the whole person; don't just stare into his or her eyes.

➤ Show interest by your facial expressions. Smile or show concern when appropriate.

➤ Indicate that you are following the conversation by nods or gestures.

➤ Ask questions about what's being said. You can paraphrase "So the way I understand it is …" or ask specific questions about specific points. This technique not only enables you to clarify points that may be unclear but also keeps you alert by making you pay full attention.

➤ Don't interrupt. A pause should not be a signal for you to start talking. Wait.

➤ Be an empathetic listener. Listen with your heart as well as your head. Try to feel what other people are feeling when they speak. In other words, put yourself in the speaker's shoes.

Six Strategies to Become a Better Listener

You can become a better listener by keeping in check some of the main causes of ineffective listening, before they begin. All you have to do is make a few changes in your work environment and in your approach to listening:

1. Set your voice mail to pick up all phone calls right away. One of the most common distractions is probably the telephone. You want to give the speaker your full attention.

Answering the phone not only interrupts your discussion but also disrupts the flow of thoughts. Even after you've hung up, your mind may still be pondering over the call. If shutting off the phone isn't feasible, get away from the telephone. Go to an empty conference room. Even if there is a phone in the room, it probably won't ring as no one knows that you're there.

2. Hide the papers. If your desk is strewn with paper, your eyes will probably skim over them and before you realize you're reading a letter or a memo instead of listening. If you go to a conference room, take only the papers that are related to the discussion. If you must stay at your desk, put the papers in a drawer so that you won't be tempted to read them.

3. Don't get too comfortable. Robert L. tells of a particularly embarrassing situation: "Some years ago I was discussing a situation with another manager. As was my custom, I sat in my comfortable executive chair with my hands behind my head. Maybe I rocked a little, but fortunately, I caught myself before I dozed off. Ever since then, rather than taking a relaxing position when I engage in a discussion, I've made a point of sitting on the edge of my chair and leaning forward rather than backward when engaged in a discussion. This position not only brings me physically closer to the other person, but also enables me to be more attentive, and helps me to maintain eye contact. It also shows the other person that I'm truly interested in getting the full story he or she is relating and that I take seriously what is being said. And because I'm not quite so comfortable, there's less tendency to daydream."

4. Don't think about your rebuttal. It's tempting to pick up one or two points that the speaker is making and plan how you would respond to them. Do this and you'll probably miss much of the balance of what is being said, often, the really important matters. Concentrate on what is being said through the entire process.

5. Be an empathetic listener. Don't confuse empathy with sympathy. Empathy is putting yourself in the other person's shoes, so you know how he or she feels. Sympathy is feeling sorry for the situation a person faces. An empathetic listener will obtain a deeper understanding of what the speaker truly wants to convey.

6. Take notes. It's impossible to remember everything that is being said in a lengthy discussion. Even if you use shorthand, making lengthy notes keeps you from fully listening. Just jot down key words or phrases. Write down figures or important facts, just enough to help you remember. Immediately after a meeting, while the information is still fresh in your mind, write a detailed summary. Dictate it into a recorder, enter it into your computer, or write it in your notebook, whichever is best for you.

When dealing with people, remember you are not dealing with creatures of logic, but creatures of emotion.

Dale Carnegie

Seven Types of Listeners

Listeners often fall into one of the following categories:

The "Pre-occupieds"

These people come across as rushed and are constantly looking around or doing something else. Also known as multitaskers, these people cannot sit still and listen.

If you are a preoccupied listener, make a point to set aside what you are doing when someone is speaking to you.

If you are dealing with a preoccupied listener, you might want to ask: "Is this a good time?" or say: "I need your undivided attention for just a moment." Begin with a statement that would get their attention; be brief, and get to the bottom line quickly because their attention span is short.

The "Out-to-Lunchers"

These people are physically present, but mentally they are not. You can tell this by the blank look on their face. They are either daydreaming or thinking about everything and anything else but what you are saying.

If you are an out-to-luncher, act like a good listener. Be alert, maintain eye contact, lean forward, and show interest by asking questions.

If you are dealing with an out-to-luncher, check in with them every now and then to ask if they understood what you have said. As with the "pre-occupieds," begin with a statement that will catch their attention; be concise and to the point because their attention span is short.

The "Interrupters"

These people are ready to chime in at any given time. They are perched and ready for a break to complete your sentence for you. They are not listening to you but focused instead on what they want to say.

If you are an interrupter, make a point to apologize every

time you catch yourself interrupting. This would make you more conscious of it.

If you are dealing with an interrupter, when they come in, stop immediately and let them talk, or they would never listen to you. When they are done, you might say, "as I was saying before..." and then continue making your point.

The "Whatevers"

These people remain aloof and show little emotion while listening. They give off the impression that they are not at all interested in what you are talking about.

If you are a "whatever," concentrate on the full message, not just the verbal message. Make a point to listen with your eyes, ears, and heart.

If you are dealing with a "whatever," dramatize your ideas and ask questions to get their involvement.

The "Combatives"

These people are armed and ready for war. They enjoy disagreeing and blaming others.

If you are a "combative" listener, make an effort to put yourself in the speaker's shoes and understand, accept, and find merit in their point of view.

While dealing with this type of listener, when they disagree or resort to blaming: if the criticism is correct, thank them and take appropriate action; if it is not, rather than arguing, tell them you appreciate their suggestions and then go on with the balance of your message.

The "Analysts"

These people constantly take on the role of counselors or

therapists and are ready to provide you with answers even when you have not asked. They think they are great listeners and love to help. They are constantly in an-analyze-what-you-are-saying and fix-it mode.

If you are an "analyst," relax and understand that not everyone is looking for an answer, solution, or advice. Some people just like bouncing ideas off others to help them see the answers more clearly themselves.

If you are dealing with an analyzer, you might want to begin by saying: "I just need to run something by you, I'm not looking for any advice."

The "Engagers"

These are the consciously aware listeners. They listen with their eyes, ears, and hearts, and try to put themselves in the speaker's shoes. This is listening at the highest level. Their listening skills encourage you to continue talking and gives you the opportunity to discover your own solutions and let your ideas unfold.

> You can close more business in two months by becoming interested in other people than you can in two years by trying to get people interested in you.
>
> —Dale Carnegie

Watch the Body Language

All of us convey information with more than the words we use. What we say is often modified by the way we use our body, our facial expressions, our gestures, the way we sit or stand.

Wouldn't it be great if we could buy a dictionary of body

language so that we could look up what each gesture or expression mean? Then we could interpret what everybody is really saying.

Some people have tried to write such "dictionaries" that lists a variety of different "signals" and identify their meanings. For example, if the other person strokes his chin, "what could it mean?" "Ha! I know. He's pondering about the situation." Indeed, he may very well be thinking it over, but it might also mean that he didn't shave this morning and his chin itches.

The person across from you is sitting with her arms folded in front of her. Some "experts" interpret this to mean that she is holding herself in, blocking you out, rejecting you. Nonsense! Look at a roomful of people in a class, a lecture, or a theatrical performance. You will note that a good number of these people are sitting with arms crossed. Does that mean that they are rejecting the instructor or actors? Of course not, it's a comfortable way to sit, and if you are cold, it keeps you warm. On the other hand, if in the middle of a conversation, the other party should suddenly cross their arms, it might mean that at that point they are disagreeing with you.

There is No Universal Body Language

The fact that one cannot read body language indicates that there is no universal body language. Each of us has his or her own way of expressing ideas, feelings and nuances, nonverbally.

Why should this be? Body language is an acquired trait. We tend to imitate other people. It starts with our parents and is often closely tied in with our ethnic background. Two boys are born in Detroit, Michigan, but their parents immigrated to the United States from two different countries. One family came from a country where the usual way to express oneself was with gesticulation—you could not speak the language without using your hands. The other family came from a country where nobody gesticulated except when highly emotional. The two boys met for the first time in high school. The first boy was discussing a situation in his usual way—his hands moving wildly. The second boy thought: "My goodness, he's excited about this." When he responded in his usual quiet way, the first boy thought: "He's not even interested."

Cultural differences also affect the way one uses nonverbal communications.

Following the theft of money from a high school cafeteria in New York City, the principal interviewed all of the students who had access to the cash register. After the interviews he determined that the thief was a Latin-American girl and he suspended her. A social worker visited the principal about this and asked why he felt she was the thief. He responded: "All the other students looked me straight in the eye and said that they didn't do it. This girl wouldn't look me in the eye. She looked down at her toes throughout the interview. She's obviously guilty."

The social worker said: "Mr Principal, a well bred Latin-American girl is taught never to look straight into the eyes of an exalted personage as the principal, but to look demurely to the ground when talking to him." The cultural difference generated the body language and was misinterpreted by the principal.

A similar pattern may be determined by family habits. When anybody speaks to a member of Esther's family, they respond with frequent nods of their head. Most of us would interpret this to mean that they were agreeing with us. But as Esther pointed out when questioned about this—all it meant to them was that they have acknowledged what was being said.

Study Each Person's Use of Nonverbal Clues

If body language is an important aspect of communication, is there any way that we can learn to read it? There is no one hundred percent approach to reading body language. The only way to obtain a reasonably good interpretation of a person's nonverbal actions and reactions is to know the person with whom you are communicating. When you deal with the same people over and over again, by careful observation you can learn to read their body language. You note that when Claudia agrees with you, she tends to lean forward and when Paul agrees he tilts his head to the right. You observe that Esther nods no matter what you say, but when she is not sure of something, she has a puzzled look on her face even though she is nodding.

By making careful mental notes about each of the people with whom you communicate, you would be able to understand their nonverbal clues and interpret them properly. After a while, you may note that some gestures or expressions are more common among certain people you communicate with than others. From these you may make some generalizations when dealing with new people, but you must be careful not to put too much credence in those interpretations until you have had more experience with these people.

When the body language seems to contradict or skew the meaning of the words being spoken, or you are not sure what the signal being sent really means—ask a question. Get the person to communicate verbally what he or she really meant. By good questioning, you can overcome the doubts that the nonverbal actions induced and be able to deal with them.

The Feedback Loop

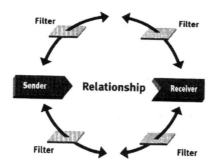

Good listeners recognize that communication is like a two-way radio. The sender sends a message to the receiver and the receiver responds. At that moment, the receiver has become the sender and the sender the receiver. In all of our communications, whether with friends and family, in social and community activities or on the job, we are constantly changing roles from sender to receiver and back again. Unless we recognize that we are always playing this dual role, our messages may degenerate into a one-person diatribe where no real communication would take place.

Just as in any radio interchange, static may develop between the sender's radio and receiver's radio causing distortion in the message. They filter the message so that what was received was not exactly the same message that was sent. This is more likely to occur when the message is long, or deals with complex matter. These distortions may emanate from the sender or from the receiver.

How Has the Message Been Received

In communication we alternate between being senders and receivers. We must be good listeners not only when we are the receiver, but also when we send a message, we must assure that the receiver has listened to what we have sent.

This is how it works: The sender sends a message to the receiver; the receiver responds. When this response is received, the sender, who has now become the receiver, filters this response through the mind's computer, which has been programmed to seek out clues as to how the message has been received. If what was sent was not what was received, a correction can be made in the next message.

> Myra: "Mike, I need to know what equipment is available, what material is in stock, time estimates and what people will be assigned to the project."
> Mike: "We have all the materials we need and we can get the job started on Monday."
> Myra: "Fine, but I still need the figures on each of the items I mentioned so I can write my report."

When Mike received Myra's message, his mindset was geared to getting the job started. Myra's objective was to obtain information for her report. The message was distorted by the perception each had of the purpose of the communication. This was corrected by Myra's next response. She picked up the clue and acted upon it.

Ask Questions

It is not always easy to pick up all the clues. To augment this—ask questions. After every four or five exchanges, ask a question to obtain reaction to what has been covered till that point.

"What problems do you anticipate may develop if we do it this way?"

"How much additional time will your people need to complete this phase?"

From the answers to your questions, you would be able to pick up additional clues and make necessary adjustments.

When the matters involved are complex, to be sure that the message has been received and understood, ask a few specific questions regarding the key points. This would help to quickly identify problem areas and provide immediate clarifications.

Observe Nonverbal Clues

Dr. Kim P., chief engineer of a technical facility, cautions: "My people are professionals and highly knowledgeable in their fields. They tend to rush ahead of me and anticipate what I would say. Often they are right, but there are times when they turn me off before I am finished, assuming they know what I am going to tell them. To overcome this I watch their nonverbal language carefully—their eyes, their facial expressions, their body language. If it appears to me that they are no longer listening, I stop talking for a few seconds and after a pause, ask a specific question on what I said. This brings them back on track."

Loren supervises several people who have limited knowledge of the English language. She depends on observing body language for feedback. She says: "If I see a blank expression on their face, I know I didn't get my message across. I repeat it in simpler words and demonstrate non-verbally what has to be done."

When You are the Receiver

When your boss is giving instructions and you are not sure just what is meant, create your own feedback loop—ask questions.

Don't wait till the end of the discussion, when he or she asks: "Do you have any questions?" All through the discussion, at appropriate moments, ask questions related to what has just been brought up.

It may be in the form of paraphrase: "So the way you want this to be done is…" restating in your own words how you have interpreted the instruction. If it is wrong, it can be clarified, and if it is right, immediate approval will reinforce it.

In some cases a specific question on a specific point will augment your interpretation and avert errors that could have been made. By the end of the discussion, not only would you have a clear picture of what has to be done, but your boss would know that you have followed the instructions.

Sum and Substance

To be an effective listener:

> Listen empathetically. Try to feel what the other person is feeling when he or she speaks.
> Remove all distractions. Turn off the telephone; remove all papers not pertinent to the conversation.
> Clarify any uncertainties after he or she has spoken. Make sure you understood what was said by rephrasing what you heard.

- Try to honestly see things through the other person's point of view.
- Don't jump to conclusions or make assumptions. Keep an open and accepting attitude.
- Show interest by your facial expressions. Smile or show concern when appropriate.
- Indicate that you are following the conversation by nods or gestures.
- Ask questions about what is being said. You can paraphrase, "So the way I understand it is..." or you can ask specific questions about specific points. This not only enables you to clarify points, but keeps you alert and paying full attention.
- Don't interrupt! A pause should not be interpreted as a time for you to start talking—wait.
- Observe the speaker's body language.
- Use the feedback loop. What is said may not be what was received. Search out filters and overcome them. To get back on track, restate your point or ask pertinent questions.

4

SPEAKING WITH CONFIDENCE
AND CONVICTION

When surveys were made concerning people's fears, speaking in public invariably appeared on the top of the list. Unlike some of the other fears, such as death, disease, or loss of job, overcoming the public speaking phobia is relatively easy.

Dale Carnegie expressed this most succinctly:

Is there any faintest shadow of a reason why you should not be able to think as well in a perpendicular position before an audience as you can sitting down? Is there any reason you should pay host to butterflies in your stomach and become a victim of the "trembles" when you get up and address an audience? Surely, you realize that this condition can be remedied, that training and practice will wear away your audience fright and give you self-confidence.

Preparation—The First Step for Successful Talks

In making a public speech, it is essential to be well prepared. How to do this in a business situation will be discussed in the next chapter. If, however, we are asked to talk to our child's class, a meeting of a community association, or any other group and have to choose a topic, the best route is to talk about something that we know and realize that we know. Don't spend ten minutes or ten hours preparing a talk; spend ten weeks or ten months—better still, spend ten years.

Talk about something that has aroused your interest; that you have a deep desire to communicate to your listeners.

Dale Carnegie tells the story of one of his class members, Gay K. Gay who had never made a speech in public before she enrolled in Mr. Carnegie's public speaking course.

She was terrified. She feared that public speaking might be an obscure art far beyond her abilities. Yet at the fourth session of the course, as she made an impromptu talk, she held the audience spellbound. She was asked to speak on, "The Biggest Regret of My Life." Gay then made a talk that was deeply moving. The listeners could hardly keep the tears back. Even Mr. Carnegie could hardly keep the tears from welling up in his own eyes. Her talk went like this:

"The biggest regret of my life is that I never knew a mother's love. My mother died when I was only a year old. I was brought up by a succession of aunts and other relatives who were so absorbed in their own children that they had no time for me. I never stayed with any of them very long. They were always sorry to see me come and glad to see me go. They never took any interest in me or gave me any affection. I knew

I wasn't wanted. Even as a little child I could feel it. I often cried myself to sleep because of loneliness. The deepest desire of my heart was to have someone ask to see my report card from school. But no one ever did. No one cared. All I craved as a little child was love—and no one ever gave it to me."

Had Gay spent ten years preparing that talk? No. She had spent twenty years. She had been preparing herself to make that talk when she cried herself to sleep as a little child. She had been preparing herself to make that talk when her heart ached because no one asked to see her report card from school. No wonder she couldn't talk about that subject. She could not have erased those early memories from her mind. Gay had rediscovered a storehouse of tragic memories and feelings hidden away deep down inside her. She didn't have to pump them up. She didn't have to work at making that talk. All she had to do was to let her pent-up feelings and memories rush up to the surface like oil from a well.

Speakers who talk about what life has taught them never fail to keep the attention of their listeners.

Dale Carnegie

Preparing a Talk When the Subject is Unfamiliar

Often, we could be asked to speak on a subject in which we have little or no experience. This generally occurs while making a business presentation. The purpose of most of these presentations is to get action of some kind—a commitment to purchase from a customer, the next step in the midst of a long project, a decision to change direction—all examples of common presentations.

In preparing this type of communication, begin with the end in mind—i.e., the action you want your listeners to take—and work back from that point. Then, when we would make the presentation, we seek an example or incident, which will capture attention and prepare the way for the desired action. By vividly reconstructing an incident we can make it the basis of influencing the conduct of others. It would be the evidence that convinces the audience to act. In communicating the example, we must recreate a segment of our experience in such a way that it tends to have the same effect on our listeners as it originally had on us. This would prepare us to clarify, intensify, and dramatize our points in a way that will make them interesting and compelling to listen to.

Following which we must obtain from research as much information as we can. A good presenter should know ten times as much about the subject than what would be necessary in the talk. Develop evidence to support your points. Effective use of evidence will be discussed in chapter 6.

Finally, prepare the conclusion. The way we end the presentation has been proven to be one of the best methods to motivate listeners to act. We will see that the end of the presentation yields positive results-especially, from the audience's point of view.

The Magic Formula for Dynamic Talks

We can avoid making rambling, incoherent, boring talks by using a simple, easy to apply three-step approach. This approach magically transforms our presentation into a vibrant, forceful speech.

The magic formula consists of three steps:

Incident: By citing an incident or an anecdote that illustrates the point that you plan to make is a sure-fire way to get and hold the attention of your listeners.

Action: Following an anecdote, point out what course of action you would want the audience to take.

Benefit: Conclude by showing how this action will benefit the audience.

If we wish to persuade others, we must be alert and alive ourselves. We must speak with sincerity and excitement. We must speak as to make our listeners feel that we believe in every word we say.

Incident

When delivering your report, always begin with the incident. Why? The incident captures the immediate attention of your listeners and makes the communication more conversational.

When using the Magic Formula, be sure that both your *action* and *benefit* steps are brief, clear, and specific. The incident must be based on an experience that taught you a lesson. Remember, your point must communicate what action you want your listeners to take. The more specific the *action* step, the better. To communicate clearly, identify one specific action and one specific benefit.

Action (Point)

The second step of the Magic Formula, the action, is what we want the audience to execute. It may be to buy our product, to write to the congressman, to stop smoking, or just to think more about the subject. Invest at least three times more time in preparing than you will in the delivery of your message.

Benefit

The third step of the Magic Formula, the benefit is what the listeners would receive by doing what is asked for in the action step.

For example, "By using this component, you will reduce the time spent and lower the cost in manufacturing your (name the product)."

"Quitting smoking will not only make you healthier and enable you to live longer, but will keep your families from the dangers of passive smoking."

Speak from the Listener's Point of View

Our ability to inspire others to embrace change is largely dependent on our ability to communicate from our listeners' point of view. Early in the presentation, we must build the trust of our listeners. Getting favorable attention and establishing the need to consider change must be accomplished quickly. The use of an incident is an effective way to do this. To be convinced, they must see the evidence that clearly—from their point of view—supports the need for change. The audience must not feel that they are being forced to change—they must see change as the logical option.

After establishing the need for change, we must illustrate both the advantages and disadvantages of each alternative. We should be are careful and ensure that the alternatives are considered from the point of view of our listeners and that they are designed and communicated in a credible and balanced fashion.

We must conclude with evidence to support that our belief is the best alternative and state what action should be taken and what would the benefits be for them. Thereby inspiring our listeners to embrace the specific change that will yield the desired results.

How to Prepare and Deliver Talks

Here are eight principles that will help immensely in preparing talks:

1. Make brief notes of the interesting things that you want to mention.
2. Don't write down the talks. If you do, we would be using written language instead of easy, conversational language; and when you would stand up to talk, you would probably find yourself trying to remember what you wrote down. That will keep you from speaking naturally and with spark.
3. Never, never, never memorize a talk word by word. If you memorize the talk, you are almost sure to forget it; and the audience would probably be glad, for nobody wants to listen to a canned speech. Even if you don't forget it, it would sound crammed. You would have a faraway look in your eyes and a faraway ring in your voice.
4. During a longer talk, if you are afraid that you would forget what you want to say, make some brief notes and glance at them occasionally.
5. Fill the talk with illustrations and examples. By far the easiest way to make a talk interesting is to fill it with examples.

6. Tell stories and anecdotes to illustrate the points. Tell how you or someone you know enforced that point. Give specific examples that you learned from research on the subject.

7. Become an authority on the subject. Develop that priceless asset known as *reserve power*. Know ten times more about the subject than what is required during the talk.

8. Rehearse the talk by conversing with friends—not necessarily a dress rehearsal, but try out the points of view that would be made during the conversation with others to get their reaction. This would enable you to discover how your jokes would be received, and which remark would elicit people's interest. This provides a reaction that is obviously not possible from just rehearsing a talk in front of a mirror.

Add Power to the Incident

To communicate effectively, we must use more than just our voice. We must also use animation or gestures. In other words—use the entire body. Natural, effective, and spontaneous gestures are extremely powerful for two reasons:

›   Gestures stimulate and inspire the speaker. It wakes them up, loosens and relaxes them. By using gestures, we let ourselves go physically, mentally, and emotionally.

›   Gestures also impact the listener. The emotional effect gestures have on a listener is both obvious and at times, even dramatic. Just think about some of the world's greatest communicators. In almost every case the use of natural, spontaneous gestures contributed to the effectiveness of the speaker and the impact of his or her message.

Be careful in how you use your body before an audience.

> Don't stand with legs and arms crossed.
> Don't place any barriers across your body such as a purse, papers, or a coffee cup.
> Don't stand with your feet spread apart.
> Don't cross arms in front of the body or at sides.
> Don't hold your head down with your eyes on the lectern (reading the script).
> Do hold your head straight, put your chin up, and chest out.
> Do hold your shoulders back.
> Do maintain eye contact with the group.
> Do smile appropriately.

Since most of us lose the spontaneity and naturalness of youth as we grow older, we tend to slip into a definite mold of physical and vocal communication. We find ourselves less ready to use gestures and animation ... In short, we lose the freshness and spontaneity of a true conversation.

Dale Carnegie

Five Steps for Better Articulation

For some people poor articulation reduces the effectiveness of their speech—and often many of us do not really know how we sound to other people. We do not hear ourselves as others hear us. As noted in the discussion of the telephone voice, only by listening to a careful recording of our speech that we can truly appreciate how we really sound. But, if we were to read into a recorder several paragraphs from a magazine, it would not be realistic. We must tape our voice without being aware it is being taped. A simple way to do this is to place a voice-activated tape recorder on your desk for a day. All our conversations that day—whether in person or on the telephone will be recorded. Listen to them and find out if you have any speech problems.

Improve Articulation

Danny is a supervisor. When he gives orders or instructions to his people, he mumbles. His words come across indistinctly and it is difficult to understand what he says. But his people are too embarrassed to tell him that he is mumbling, so they guess what he means—and often guess wrong. This results in errors, missed deadlines, and other problems.

Carrie is very bright. She thinks fast and speaks too fast because she's always trying to keep up with her thoughts. Unfortunately, her listeners cannot keep up with her and miss a good deal of what she says.

Darryl is just the opposite. He speaks very slowly. Although it is easy to understand what he is saying, his listeners often jump ahead of him, anticipating what they think he intends to say—often incorrectly.

Terry, Merry and Jerry interject extra sounds, words or phrases into their speech. Terry adds "er" to every word; Merry interjects, "Y'know" after every phrase and Jerry punctuates each sentence with "OK!" We call these and similar detracting sounds or expressions "word whiskers."

These are some of the most common problems in articulation. Most of the people who have these problems do not even realize they speak that way. By listening to tape recordings of their voices, they become aware that they are mumbling, speaking too fast or too slow or are adding sounds, words or phrases to their sentences.

All that is needed to correct these problems is awareness, and a careful listening to one's speech will do this. When people become aware that they mumble, they would make an effort to stop it. When a person knows that every fifth word uttered is "y'know," he or she will stop saying it.

Overcome Speech Defects

If a person has a serious speech defect like a stutter or a stammer, the chances are that he or she avoids situations that call for much oral communication. However, much has been learned in recent years to help such people. A well-known example is Anne Glenn, the wife of Senator John Glenn, who overcame a major stuttering problem and when her husband ran for office, made campaign speeches for him.

Ivan immigrated to the United States from Russia, and although he had learned English in his native land, his accent was very difficult for Americans to understand. A skilled engineer, he was stymied in his career growth because of this speech problem. At the suggestion of a career counselor, he sought the help of a speech therapist. In less than a year, Ivan's speech improved so much that he was promoted to a managerial position where he had to communicate with executives both within and outside of his company.

Speech therapy is available in universities and can be most helpful for people with speech defects of all sorts or difficult to understand foreign accents.

Tone is Critical

Claude speaks in a monotone. It is not difficult to understand what Claude is saying. His diction is very good. However, it is difficult to sustain one's attention because he has not learned to use inflection and modulation in his voice. People who speak in a monotone cannot hold the interest of their listeners. As in other speech problems, the speakers do not realize that they speak in a monotone. Listening to their own conversations would bring this to their attention and once aware, they could make efforts to overcome it.

Select Appropriate Tempo

The speed in which we speak also affects the message. If we wish to convey urgency or excitement, it is best to increase the tempo. If we speak slowly when we tell people that they should better work faster or they won't meet a deadline, we will not generate the sense of urgency that is required.

On the other hand, if we want something to sink in, we should say it more slowly. "We've had too many complaints about the quality of our work, if each of you would take one more minute to check your work, this could be overcome."

Control Voice Volume

Raising and lowering one's voice in a spoken message is the equivalent of adding italics to a printed page. Whether the voice ought to be raised or lowered, depends on the context of the message.

Careful: It is tempting to shout when one wants to emphasize a point. Shouting can be distracting or could even convey a negative message. Volume should be controlled so that we never speak too loudly or too softly. If we know we have a loud voice, it is especially important to control the volume. This is particularly important in public speeches where a microphone may be in use. Too high a volume can easily distort one's voice when amplified. Whether the voice is naturally soft or loud, careful attention to how it comes across and serious practice in projecting it can aid us in controlling the volume.

Whether we are speaking privately or publicly, if we follow these suggestions, we would easily be understood and would also make a more favorable impression on our listeners.

Twelve Ways to Make Our Listeners Like Us

In order to achieve an empathetic hearing of our messages, we must make our listeners like us. Here are twelve tested principles for winning listeners and influencing audiences.

1. *Consider yourself honored by being asked to address an audience—and say so!* Regardless of its size or type, it is nearly always a compliment to be asked to speak to a group. It is a matter of courtesy and good manners to acknowledge such a compliment. That is one way to make an audience like us.

2. *Appreciate your listeners sincerely.* Never speak before any group without finding out as much as you can about that group, beforehand. Then, spend a few seconds reminding the audience of some of its fine or unusual qualities that makes you proud to be chosen as its speaker.

3. *Whenever possible, mention the names of a few listeners.* A person's name is the sweetest sound in any language;

so, whenever possible, mention the names of a few people present in the audience. Note when political figures speak at a meeting, they almost always mention the names of local officials who are in the audience.

4. *Play yourselves down—not up.* Modesty usually inspires confidence and goodwill. For example, Abraham Lincoln was a master at this. One night during the Lincoln-Douglas debates, Lincoln was serenaded by a brass band; and as he stepped out into the dimly lit porch of the hotel to speak to the band, someone held up a lantern so that the crowd could see Lincoln's homely face. Lincoln began by saying: "My friends, the less you see of me the better you will like me." Lincoln knew the wisdom of the biblical advice: "He that humbles himself shall be exalted."

5. *Say "we"—not "you."* Never assume a condescending attitude towards the listeners. Bring all of them into the talk by using "we" instead of "you."

   The speaker says: "When *you* are worried, *you* ought to get so busy that *you* won't have time to think about *your* troubles." If he or she keeps repeating "you," the impression is that the speaker is lecturing and talking down to the audience.

   Instead say: "When we are worried, *we* ought to get so busy that *we* won't have time to think about *our* troubles." See the difference? When we use the word "you," we make ourselves offensive by seeming to take a superior attitude. A note of caution: The exclusive use of "we" tends to make a speaker sound equally condescending.

6. *Don't talk with a scowling face and an upbraiding voice.* Remember that the expression on your face and the tone of

your voice often speak louder than your words. Regardless of whether you are talking in private or public, you can't win friends with a scowling face and a scolding voice.

There is old Chinese proverb that we ought to cut out and paste inside our hats. It goes like this:

"A man without a smiling face must not open a shop."

Dale Carnegie

7. *Talk in terms of your listeners' interests.* All listeners are intensely and eternally interested in themselves and how to solve their problems. That is about all they are interested in. So, if you show them how to be happier, how to make more money, how to stop worrying and how to get what they want, they will listen to you gladly—regardless of what kind of voice we have, how we breathe, stand, look, gesture or what kind of grammar we use.

For example, when asked how did she manage to win friends so easily and become a more interesting conversationalist, a sales manager reported that she merely asked people, "How did you get into your line of work?" Then she centered her conversation on the response she received. She declared that this simple question had worked wonders for her, especially with strangers. Before addressing a group, find out what their main concerns are and allude to them in the talk.

8. *Have a good time while making the talk.* Unless we enjoy speaking, can we even hope that people would enjoy listening? No matter what our mental and emotional attitudes are, they are bound to be contagious. If we are

having a good time speaking, singing or skating, the people who are watching us or listening to us are also bound to have a good time. Emotional attitudes are as contagious as measles.

One may ask: "How can I have a rip-roaring good time making a talk?" The secret is simple: talk about something you have earned the right to talk about, something that puts sparkle in your eyes and feeling in your voice.

9. *Don't apologize.* We've all heard speakers begin by saying something like this: "I didn't know I was supposed to give this talk until two weeks ago, when the chairman told me I would have to fill in for the president." How about this opening remark? "Unaccustomed as I am to public speaking…" some speakers apologize before even starting. We should never accept an invitation to speak unless we are able to give it the necessary preparation. If we do the best we can do, no apologies are required. If we don't, no amount of apologizing will be acceptable. Apologies are usually an irritating waste of an audience's time.

However, if we are unavoidably late due to a grounded plane, a late train or some equally valid reason, we could explain the circumstances briefly and apologize courteously, and then get on with the talk before any more time is lost.

10. *Appeal to the nobler emotions of the audience.* To inspire an audience by stirring great emotions is not easy. We must first be deeply stirred ourselves. However, we are not often stirred that deeply. To align others to your way of thinking, show them how what you are proposing will in some way enable them to take part in repairing the world. Give them an example: When Susan Earl was soliciting

contributions to her favorite charity, "Heifer, International" she told how just by giving a small donation would enable a family in India to purchase a goat, which would provide milk for their children and a small income from selling the surplus.

Once this spark of noble emotion is lit and the flame plays over the speaker and the audience alike—the warm glow of this experience would be long remembered.

This is the age of dramatization. Merely stating a truth isn't enough. The truth has to be made vivid, interesting, and dramatic. You have to use showmanship. The movies do it. TV does it. And you will have to do it if you want attention.

Dale Carnegie

11. *Welcome the criticism—instead of resenting it.* Probably no other scientist who ever lived was criticized and denounced so outrageously as Charles Darwin, for his theory of evolution. Yet, he never uttered a harsh word against any of his critics. Instead, he thanked them saying that the primary purpose of his life was to uncover knowledge and discover truth, and when searching for truth, two minds were better than one. "If I am wrong," he said, "the sooner I am knocked on the head and annihilated, so much the better."

12. *Be sincere.* All the eloquence in the world would not make up for the lack of sincerity and integrity. To make the audience like you, you must inspire them with confidence in the honesty of your purpose. They may not agree with

your ideas, but they must respect your belief in those ideas if you are to be effective.

Welcome any criticism and respond with respect and humility. What we are speaks more loudly than what we say. Sincerity, integrity, modesty and unselfishness affect an audience deeply.

We prefer a clumsy speaker who radiates honesty and unselfishness to a polished orator who tries to impress us with their eloquence.

Introducing and Thanking a Speaker

If we chair a meeting or serve on a committee that has invited a speaker, we would probably be called to introduce the speaker. The introduction serves as a means of separating what has come before from what is about to be presented. It sets the stage for the audience to give its full attention to the person being introduced and the subject they will present.

The introduction also serves to identify the common ground between speaker and audience. It prepares the audience to accept the speaker because of his or her credentials and the relationship between what the speaker would offer and what the audience is interested in hearing. This is called the T-I-S method.

T—First, mention the *title* or *topic* of the presentation.

I—Identify why this topic is important or of *interest* to the audience.

S—Present the qualifications of the *speaker*. Make sure the qualifications mentioned establish the speaker's credibility to speak on the topic being presented; followed by the name of the speaker.

Preparing an Introduction

The TIS approach is not only an effective way to introduce a speaker, but could also be used if you are asked to address a group. Prepare a written introduction. Be sure it is printed or typed in large enough letters so that it can be read easily from the rostrum.

Present the introduction to the person who will be giving it well in advance of the presentation. Ask the person to read it over. Answer any questions that might arise. Encourage the person who would be introducing you to be brief, positive, and excited about the introduction.

Introducing Yourself

When we must introduce ourselves, the sequence of events changes. The first item would be our name and company or organization affiliation. Next would be the topic of the talk and its importance to the audience. In presenting your qualifications, indicate those aspects of your background that are relevant to the topic and the occasion.

Thanking a Presenter

As the chair of a meeting, we could find ourselves in a position to express our appreciation to the speakers for their presentations. Thank the speaker by acknowledging their contribution or the value of their message to the audience. The procedure should be succinct. You would be basically extending thanks on behalf of the entire group.

Guidelines for Thanking a Speaker Using the T I F Method

T—First, *thank* the presenter using their name.

I—Next, cite one specific area of *interest* from the presentation that made an impression on the audience.

F—Finally, make a *formal statement* thanking the speaker and again using their full name.

Sum and Substance

Keys to an Effective Talk:

- Learn as much as possible about the group being addressed.
- Know at least ten times more about the subject than required during the talk.
- Start with an incident that will illustrate the key point(s).
- Present evidence to substantiate the point(s).
- Pay attention to articulation, grammar, tone and tempo.
- Include animation and vocal variety.
- State clearly the action that the listeners ought to take.
- Point out the benefits of taking this action to them.
- Be prepared to respond to challenging questions.
- Maintain professional composure under pressure.
- Communicate clear, concise, positive messages.
- Sell strategic ideas to the organization.
- Communicate with competence and confidence.

5

....

MAKING GREAT PRESENTATIONS
TO GROUPS

The purpose of most business presentations is to get action of some kind. It may be a commitment to purchase from a customer, a decision to change a practice or procedure, acceptance of a plan or project, or similar actions. Even those presentations that seem to be simple "updates" call for some decision or action from someone.

To get the results we seek from our communication, our presentation must be well prepared. It must begin in a way that creates and holds the interest of our audience and end in a way that is clear and motivational.

Who is the Audience?

It is as difficult to satisfy the unknown expectations of an audience as it is to hit an unseen target. Even though it can be done, it is a risky way to seek success. Part of the process of preparation is doing research to gather the following information about the audience:

Knowledge

Find out how much the audience knows about the subject. Ask yourself: "Is the audience better informed than I am?" Never face an audience unprepared, but also never fall into the trap of assuming that the listeners are ignorant and therefore, talking down to them.

Stanley L., an attorney, began his presentation to his supervisors at the City National Bank on the changes recently made in the labor law with a detailed statement of the new provisions. He noticed that his audience seemed bored and restless. At the first break, he spoke to some of the people and learned that they had recently attended a seminar on this. Had Stanley made the effort to learn what previous exposure the supervisors had in this area, he would not have had chosen to give so much time to the basics, but instead to the legal ramifications—aspects that they had not covered in their previous training.

Expertize

The skill level and sophistication of the audience is also important because that may determine our position on the issue. If the audience is made up of people with professional or technical backgrounds, the speaker can tailor the presentation to their level. If the participants in the meeting are mostly workers with specialized training, the speaker can prepare examples and techniques in line with their specialties.

Experience

This consideration is not only how much experience the audience has, but at what level and in what environment. Experience in a laboratory is significantly different from experience in the field or on the factory floor. They would relate better with examples and illustrations that fit in with their experiences.

Needs

In order to send the listeners home with a sense of satisfaction and a glad feeling for being present there, it is wise to address their needs. Theory is important when building evidence, but eventually you must show how the theory can be translated into action.

Wants

Similar to the needs of the audience is what the audience wants. Wants and needs are not always the same. If you only address their needs, it is difficult to satisfy an audience and move them to action.

Sally L. managed a boutique selling high priced handbags, costume jewelry, and accessories. She felt frustrated when the first speaker at the seminar she attended spoke only of the key requirements needed to operate a successful store. His suggestions were sound, but they did not excite her. However, the second speaker talked about the dreams she had about the perfect store. Sally was fully attentive and excited because they expressed not just what she needed, but the things she hopes for.

Goals

Determine the goals of the audience and keep them in mind as you plan your presentation. Before Allan L., a human resource consultant, prepared his talk on employee benefits to be presented to the H.R. staff of a client company, he discussed with the H.R. manager what short-term and long-term goals he had for the department. He was then able to gear his presentation to these goals, rather than talking in general terms.

What is the Purpose?

There are only a few purposes for a presentation. Following are the most accepted ones:

Convince

The purpose of many presentations is simply to get the audience to do something. The challenge is to persuade the audience to make a decision or to take an action.

Inform

Another logical purpose is to present information for the enlightenment of our audience. This format focuses on clarity and understanding.

Motivate

When an audience needs to change their opinion or take an unpopular action, the purpose of the presentation is to motivate. Motivation usually goes hand in hand with that of convincing.

Entertain

In one sense, every presentation should entertain. For the audience to be in a favorable frame of mind and open to being convinced, enlightened, or motivated, they need to be entertained. Entertainment is not necessarily based on humor, although that can be a big part of it. In the broadest sense, to entertain an audience is to make them glad they were there and glad we were the presenter.

What is the Message?

It hardly seems necessary to address the importance of having a message, but unfortunately sometimes presentations have no message or at least no easily discoverable message. They may be vague about the subject or there may be so many messages woven into the presentation that it is impossible to identify anything significant. Good speakers know what the message is and keep it in mind throughout the preparation, so that the presentation stays on track.

Be Creditable

As a representative of your organization speaking to a group,—be they customers, the Chamber of Commerce, a service club or a legislative committee—the impression you make determines how the audience will view your organization. Your clients or audience get an impression of your company through your ability to present the specified topics. Business audiences are reluctant to believe what is being said about a company or product unless they believe the person delivering the message.

Business people often make the mistake of overstating a company's ability by making claims, thus losing their (and their company's) credibility to perform or deliver. One must present accurate facts about one's organization. Facts should never be presented without presenting the benefits they could bring to the audience.

Opening a Presentation

The opening of a presentation differs from its content. Its distinct purpose is to elicit the audience's interest in the speaker and the message. Roger Ailes, in his book, *You are the Message*, states that we make an impression on our audience within seven seconds. Good or bad, an impression is made. In today's high-paced business world, those seven seconds are vital to gaining the trust of our audience and establishing professional credibility. If a bad first impression is made it is difficult—if not impossible—to correct it within the time of making a presentation.

With so much at stake, it is critical that our audience see us as real, believable, credible, professional, and trustworthy. Since understanding begins immediately upon opening a presentation, we must work on planning and delivering an impressive introduction. We should strive to be ourselves by being personal and natural, conveying trustworthiness and gaining the favorable interest of our audience. Start with something that will draw attention immediately. Here are some examples:

- ➤ "We all have the same amount of one very important asset—time."
- ➤ "Last year a million 'gadgets' were sold in the United States—and not a single person needed one."

Questions Based on Need or Interest

> "If there was a better way to market (name the product or service), you would be interested, wouldn't you?"
> "If I could tell you a way to avoid heart attacks, you surely would want to listen, wouldn't you?"

Mysterious Statement

> "When you fold your arms, which one is on top—the right or the left?" (This opening was used in a speech on habits and the difficulty of changing set habits.)
> "Your company's greatest asset will never show on a balance sheet!" (This was the opening to a speech regarding the value of the employees.)

Compliment

> "Your Chairman told me about your great support in improving community spirit and I congratulate you for it. What this shows about you is ..." (The beginning of a speech given to a group of co-workers in the community after a luncheon.)
> "Sincere congratulations to the 121 percent sales increase which you achieved during the last budget year! What this shows about you is ..." (Said by a sales manager at the beginning of a sales meeting.)

Note: When opening with a compliment, it is best to give a compliment that is based on something concrete or factual and not just an impression or hearsay, which could be misconstrued as insincere flattery.

Dramatic Incident

> "Last Thursday evening, as I approached my car, I observed a beautiful, sleek, red sports car race past me. All of a sudden I heard the tires screech. The brakes, firmly applied, slowed the car to a crawl as it made its way down the old gravel road with huge potholes. It then struck me that this situation was analogous to our own information system network. With some of the most contemporary softwares and equipments in the market, we are still attempting to transmit through an antiquated cabling system. It is only through a new fiber optic cabling network that we, like this beautiful sports car, will be able to capitalize upon our potential performance."

There are always three speeches for each one that you actually gave—the one you practiced, the one you gave, and the one you wish you gave.

Dale Carnegie

The Message

Once the opening has captured the attention of the audience, it is necessary to establish the theme or message of the presentation. As in a fine symphony where the composer reveals the theme and then proceeds to create variations on it, the presenter presents the message and then proceeds to develop it with facts, information, and evidence.

The opening is designed to get the attention of the audience. The message statement focuses attention on the subject. It can be a statement of intent, such as: "We are now going to examine the pros and cons of the new budget process." It can be a question such as: "What are the steps necessary to achieve a ten percent increase in market share next year?" Sometimes the message statement is presented as a proposal of logic such as: "If ... is true, then ... is also true, and ... is the natural result."

Evidence Defeats Doubt

Using evidence is an essential part of an effective presentation. Questions that often arise in the minds of audience members—even if seldom asked—are: "Why should I listen to you?" "Why should I believe you?" "Who besides you says this?" When you need to convince others of your view, one of your primary tools should be the use of evidence. How to develop and use evidence will be discussed in chapter 6.

Closing a Presentation

The opening of a presentation should create a positive first impression. Whereas, the conclusion should solidify a positive lasting impression. Some examples

Summarize in a Few Words

> "In summary, the key points to remember are ..."
> "Therefore, the action we need to take is ..."

Appeal to the Nobler Motives

> "In the interest of the company."
> "For a better society."
> "To decrease famine."
> "Your contribution can save lives."

Throw Down a Challenge

- "It is up to you."
- "You are the only ones who can realize these goals."

Dramatize Your Ideas

- A slide showing the final project.
- A picture that indicates the team's progress.
- A token or lapel pin that is distributed to the audience.

Repeat the Most Important Point

- "... we will see our goals realized."
- "... your income will be increased by X%."

Use a Motivating Statement

- "No more financial worries."
- "Imagine your children happy, healthy, and safe."
- "You can have an extra hour with your family every day."

Use a Quotation

- Use direct quotes that are relevant.
- Be familiar with whom you are quoting.

Speak on a Personal Level

- "As Susan and Betsy have demonstrated, we can achieve this level of performance."
- "If we, as a team, follow Tom and John's example, we will realize our goals."

> *There is only one way... to get anybody to do anything. And that is by making the other person want to do it.*
>
> Dale Carnegie

The Questions and Answer Period

To effectively control a Q&A period, communicate clearly, in the beginning, how much time would be allotted to question and answer. This helps keep the questions and answers short and to the point.

The rule of thumb is to keep answers short. On certain occasions, it is advantageous to take the liberty of a longer answer, particularly if there was not enough time to develop that point in the presentation. However, short answers allows for more questions.

Be sure someone from the audience does not use the questioning privilege to make a speech. If that begins to happen, gracefully ask the person to ask a question. It is also important not to let any one person dominate the questioning period. It is our responsibility to remain in control.

If we do not know the answer to a specific question, say so. Honesty gains respect.

Opening the Question and Answer Period

Applause generally follows immediately after a presentation. Then it is simply a matter of saying: "I have ten minutes for questions and answers. Who has the first question?" This request says that we expect questions, and now is the time for the first one.

An expectant look on our face and a raised hand shows the audience what to do next. Look at the person asking the question, focus, and demonstrate good listening skills. Maintain a pleasant facial expression and welcome the question. Once you have heard and understood the question, turn to the rest of the audience, and paraphrase the question. By paraphrasing, you gain some time to gather your thoughts as well as make sure everyone else has heard the question. Probably what is most important is to remain in control and make it "your" question. Restatement of the question also gives you an opportunity to take the "sting" or the "barb" out of the question, if that was the intention of a hostile member of the audience.

What can you do when no one asks a question? Sometimes after a presenter asks for questions, the audience does not respond. Most often this simply means that our listeners are unsure of how "safe" it is to ask questions. Asking a question yourself would stimulate the audience. For instance, you could say: "A question that is often asked is …" and then answer the question. Then ask: "Who has the next question?" This usually sets the stage for further questions. Don't be overly afraid of a few seconds of silence. The audience wants to fill that silence as much as you do. If however, the audience still remains silent, ask another question and answer it. Twice is enough. Thank the audience for their attention, or repeat the closing of the formal presentation.

How To Close a Question and Answer Period

When you know your time is about to run out, ask: "Who has the final question?" This signals the audience that answering questions is about to come to an end. When you have answered the final question, gracefully thank the audience for its interest, or if appropriate, repeat the closing of the formal presentation.

Use of Visuals

Using visuals can enhance a presentation, but they also introduce potential barriers that must be crossed to attain an excellent presentation. For that reason the heart of the presentation must always remain the presenter, not the visuals.

The primary purpose of visual aids is to make the presentation more understandable to the audience. Your visuals should *support* your presentation, not *be* your presentation. Visuals also add color, drama, and pacing to the presentation. Choose the visuals based on the purpose, the size of the audience, the strategy and content of the message, the availability of resources to prepare them, and the thrust of the entire presentation.

Consider Visuals When:

> Presenting data to an audience that may be difficult to grasp: If statistical material is important, trying to compare data that can't be seen is difficult, if not impossible. It can also be boring.

> Listing several items or a series of items: If they have to be compared or if sequence is vital, seeing them is essential. It helps clarify steps and aids retention.

> Explaining a complicated process: This allows the audience to follow at their own speed. Since some people grasp relationships more rapidly than others, a visual accommodates both learning styles.

Retention is important. Only about 20% of what is heard is remembered. Only 30% of what is seen is remembered, but over 50% of what is heard *and* seen is remembered. Using visuals not only makes the presentation more interesting, but it is a significant factor in how much the listeners absorb and retain.

There are various types of visuals that we can use. Select and use the type that is appropriate for the audience, the points of the presentation, and for making the greatest impact. They range from high-tech computer generated presentations all the way down to simple flip charts on chalkboards or whiteboards.

With the development of high-powered, user-friendly presentation softwares and the advances and availability of projection equipment, computer-generated presentations are becoming the norm for delivery of professional presentations. PowerPoint, from Microsoft, is frequently used today because of its simplicity and its ability to facilitate more creative visual materials.

Computer presentations can be prepared in advance or can be created in front of the audience depending on the equipment, information, and expertize of the presenter. LCD panels and portable projectors allow computer-generated presentations to be transported and presented almost anywhere.

With so many presentations being made both in the business and educational arenas, and so much data generated by and stored on computers, it is only natural that computers play a role in creating visual aids.

Formats of Visual Aids

Whether the visual is prepared on a computer or it is in another form, there are various ways in which the information can be presented:

➤ *A bar or pie graph*: Charts and graphs can emphasize and simplify large amounts of information for the listeners.

Visuals cause listeners to focus and crystallize ideas rapidly, so, well-designed charts and graphs can accelerate decision-making, often providing the side benefit of shortening meetings—usually to the delight of all.

A bar chart is best used for comparing two items, such as total earnings between years. Bar charts can also be used to compare three or four elements, such as how a company stacks up against its three closest competitors.

To represent changes over time, a line graph works well. It's effective for detailing a company's month-to-month or year-to-year performance. It also allows viewers to quickly identify trends.

When we need to show the makeup of a complex element, such as the relative sizes of various parts of a whole, a pie chart is ideal. Pie charts quickly convey a subject's overall makeup by graphically representing the proportional relationships between the parts.

> *Video:* Professionally presented examples, illustrations, and demonstrations of the highest quality are possible through the use of video. The size and economy of equipments make video presentation practical for a variety of presentational opportunities. The recording, capturing, sending, viewing, editing, and printing of video images are easy, practical, and cost effective. Video can be used for the entire presentation, or certain points can be illustrated with 5-10 minute video segments in a presentation prepared primarily around another medium. Videos on a large variety of subjects can also be bought or rented. One can check what is available online or through a library.

> *35mm Slides:* While computer-based presentations have

made 35mm slides unnecessary, many people still consider them exciting, stimulating, and practical. It is an accepted way to show full-color, three-dimensional, still pictures. Like video, slides are most effective when limited to 10-15 minute segments of the presentation.

➤ *Overhead Transparencies:* When talking to small audiences or when computer technology is not available, a simple presentation tool is the overhead projector. The transparencies are easily produced in advance and speakers can write additional material on transparencies as part of the presentation.

➤ *Flip charts:* Flip charts provide spontaneous visual support to a presentation and often contain information provided by the audience; therefore, they have a great deal of credibility. They can be prepared prior to the meeting, or they can be created in front of the audience. This semi-permanent medium can provide continual reminders of points covered throughout a meeting or training process. Sheets from the flip chart can be posted around the room so participants can refer to them when desired.

➤ *White Boards:* White porcelain boards that can be written on quietly with bright colors and erased easily have replaced the old-fashioned chalkboard. The white board's usefulness is limited by the size of the group but is helpful for spontaneous participatory activities such as brainstorming.

Handouts

Additional information and summaries can be distributed at the presentation. They are often used to provide supporting data, worksheets, outlines, or questionnaires. They should be well designed and well printed because they carry the presenter's reputation. If the handouts are intended to replace note taking, they should be distributed at the beginning of the presentation, and the audience be informed of this fact. If they are to supplement what has been presented, they should be given at the end of the presentation.

Handouts can provide more depth to the presented information. The handouts can communicate information beyond bulleted topics presented on visuals.

Information that may be of interest to the members of the audience, but cannot be covered in the allotted presentation time, like references, resources, case studies and sidebars, can also be incorporated into handouts.

Sum and Substance

Here are some of Dale Carnegie's suggestions on making presentations from his book.

Public Speaking For Success:

> The opening of a talk is highly important. It should not be left to chance. It should be carefully worked out in advance.
> Show how the thing we want people to accept is similar to something they already believe.
> Use specific instances, cite concrete examples.
> Sprinkle the talk with phrases that create pictures using words that set images floating before one's eyes.
> The conclusion of a speech is its most strategic element. What is said last is what is likely to be remembered longest.
> Summarize, restate, and outline briefly the main points that have been covered.

- Be prepared to answer questions from the audience. Repeat or paraphrase the questions before answering them.
- Appeal for action. Make sure the audience knows what you want them to do.
- Get a good ending and a good beginning and get them close together. Always stop before your audience wants you to. The point of satiation is reached soon after the peak of popularity.

6

....

GETTING THE BEST OF AN
ARGUMENT

The word *argument* can be defined in several ways. One meaning is *disagreement* in which different views are expressed, often angrily. When it comes to this definition, Dale Carnegie was correct when he wrote: "The only way to get the best of an argument is to avoid it." An angry argument can only result in a no-win situation. Another definition of *argument*, however, is *debate and discussion* about an issue. When we consider *argument* in this context, we can with preparation and skill achieve a win-win result.

Selling an idea to another person—a boss, subordinate, customer or a co-worker—is in essence an argument to persuade that person to accept what is being presented. The objective is in some way to change how that person thinks or reacts on a specific matter.

When preparing to sell an idea—whether it is to the boss or to associates—follow the principles successful salespeople use to make sale. First get the attention of the listener. One effective way to do that is to ask a challenging question. Learn what problems the person(s) to whom we are making the presentation face and focus on that. For example, if customer service is of serious concern, ask: "If there was a way to keep abreast of your customers' satisfaction without increasing your customer service staff, would you want to know about it?"

This should get their attention and now you should be ready to present evidence to show how your idea would accomplish this.

The evidence must be pertinent to the subject and of course, meaningful to the listeners. Here are seven types of evidence that have been proven to be effective. They can be remembered by the acronym *DEFEATS*—the first letter of each method:

Demonstrations (show how something works)

Examples (personal experiences or experiences of others)

Facts (points that are specific, true, and can be proven)

Exhibits (a visual, chart, graph, picture, schematic drawing, or other tangible objects)

Analogies (relating a complex idea to something simpler and easier to understand)

Testimonials of experts (quoting a recognizable or credible source)

Statistics (numbers indicating increases, decreases, percentage changes, comparisons, trends, and summations)

Those convinced against their will are of the same opinion still.

Dale Carnegie

The Twelve Rules for Disagreeing Agreeably

In dealing with others there would certainly arise situations when we would disagree with one or more of the people with whom we are interacting. Expressing disagreement need not be antagonistic. Tact, tolerance, and understanding will enable us to disagree without being disagreeable.

Rule #1: Give others the benefit of the doubt.

Maybe the person who made that outrageous generalization isn't really insensitive. Maybe this person has had a painful experience that made him or her overreact. When instead of downsizing in order to make significant reductions in expenses, it was suggested that all emloyees take a cut in salary, Susan objected vociferously. She argued that highly productive workers should not have to make a sacrifice so less productive workers' jobs could be saved.   When pressed to determine why she was so adamant, we learned that in her previous job, she had accepted a similar solution to cost-cutting, but less than a year later, she and others were terminated anyway. Only by assuring that our company was financially sound enough to avoid this could persuade Susan to change her mind.

Rule #2: Listen.

After giving someone the benefit of the doubt, listen to learn and truly understand why this person holds this belief. We must let that person know that we have heard them and are genuinely trying to see things from their perspective.

Rule #3: Take Responsibility.

When disagreeing with someone, we must always take responsibility for our own feelings. Make a commitment to respond with statements using "I." When we begin our statements with "you" it sounds as if we are blaming and confronting them; this immediately makes the other person defensive and reduces the chance of our point of view being heard.

Rule #4: Use a cushion.

Connect or "cushion" a different opinion, starting with, "I hear what you're saying ..." or "I appreciate your view on ..." Again, begin with the word "I" and not "You" or it will sound confrontational.

For example: "I understand your concern about how this might slow down the process, but I have examined all the implications of the new approach ..." Then restate how the suggested method will compensate for the initial slow-down.

Rule #5: Be Polite.

Remember that our objective is to align the other person's perspective to our own way of thinking. This can never be accomplished by being nasty or rude. Denigrating the other person by sarcasm or condescending humor will not accomplish this.

You can't win people by forcing ideas on them. Harold was an egotist who was so sure he was always right that he fought hard—no holds barred—to establish his points. He pounded the table, shouted, and antagonized his opponents by his arrogance. Such behavior not only makes everybody in the group uncomfortable, but most often results in lengthy and fruitless discussions. Even when his ideas were good, his demeanor defeated his purpose. If he had been polite and diplomatic, his excellent ideas would have been readily accepted.

Rule #6: Eliminate the word "but" or "however" from your vocabulary.

Acknowledging an individual's point of view followed by a "but" or "however" erases the acknowledgement.

Instead, use: "And..." or wait a moment silently and then, contribute your idea or opinion beginning with:

- "Let's also discuss …"
- "How about this angle …"
- "What would happen if …"
- "Have you ever thought about …"
- "Compare that idea with this idea …"
- "That's an interesting perspective."
- "I never thought about it that way."
- "I'm glad that we both agree on…."

Rule #7: State your point of view or opinion with relevant and factual evidence.

Keep emotions out of the equation by taking the time to reflect. Ask yourself: "What do I think?" "Why am I of that opinion?" "What evidence do I have to support my point?"

Rule #8: Let the other party save face.

Dale Carnegie taught us that to win friends and influence people we must always recognize and respect their individualities. When dealing with disagreements, we must never forget that. It is important to never make those who disagree with us feel inferior—even when their arguments are not valid.

Phil was one of those people who loved to point out people's errors. At meetings he would pounce on every error and gloat over his "superiority" to the person involved. Not only did that person lose face in front of his or her peers, but other members of the group also became upset. Such behavior destroys team spirit.

Rule #9: Be conscious of people's sensitivity.

Some people are very sensitive. Ashley is one of those people. She cannot accept criticism easily and becomes defensive when one of her ideas is turned down. We must be aware of this sensitivity so that we can correct or improve the situation with special care.

Instead of pointing out the areas with which we disagree, we should first compliment Ashley on all of the good points in her argument, then ask questions about the areas of disagreement. This will stimulate Ashley to rethink the situation and recognize how it can be improved.

By questioning rather that criticizing, we can get the best out of people without generating resentment. The employee rejects his or her own bad ideas and is encouraged to come up with better ones. This results in the honing of people's creative skills and obtaining more innovative ideas that would increase the effectiveness of a department.

Give consideration to other people's opinions. Let them sustain their feeling of importance.

Dale Carnegie

Rule #10: Give the other party a chance to solve the situation.

When Stephanie spoke to Harry about his frequent tardiness, she did not start with a diatribe on how lateness affects the work of the entire department and cannot be tolerated. Instead she asked: "What can you do to make it on time from now on?" By allowing Harry to come up with a solution to his own problem not only reaffirms the supervisor's faith in the employee, but also encourages employees to think about their problems and make their own decisions about them. People are more likely to follow solutions that they suggest with more commitment and enthusiasm than those superimposed on them.

There are times, particularly when the problem relates to job performance, when the supervisor must be very specific in calling attention to the employee's shortcomings. In such cases make the suggestions for improvement in positive terms. Don't say: "Your work is sloppy." It is far better to show specific examples of work that has not met standards and then ask what can be done to overcome the deficiencies. Reiterate your confidence in the employee and offer any assistance that can help.

Remember that the objective is to help the employee learn to be a better worker.

Rule #11: End on a positive note.

When Stephanie asked Harry what he can do to come in on time, he agreed to set his alarm clock at 6:15 instead of 6:30 from now on so he can avoid the occasional traffic delays that have caused his tardiness.

Stephanie agrees that this should help alleviate the problem. "Harry, I am confident that you will keep this commitment and from now on will be on time. Your contribution to our team is essential and this will assure that my confidence in you has not been misplaced."

Most importantly, give the other person support and assistance in helping them overcome whatever caused the problem. In this way, you would develop cooperative and productive relationships with people who would become valuable assets to the department.

Rule #12: Giving constructive feedback.

The effectiveness of communication can be enhanced when each party obtains honest feedback from the other. Nobody likes to be criticized, but a constructive critique, if done diplomatically, can be a significant contribution to a person's improvement.

Here are some suggestions on making feedback more acceptable:

> Get all the facts.
> Address the situation promptly and privately.
> Focus on the act or behavior, not the person.
> Give the person a genuine compliment first.
> First empathize, and then criticize. Reveal your own similar mistakes, and tell them what you did to correct them.

- Use your human relations skills. Do not order; instead ask questions and make suggestions.
- Show the benefits of changing the behavior.
- End on a friendly note and agree on how to move forward.

When you are on the receiving side of the feedback, keep in mind that the objective is to help us—not criticize us:

- Stay calm and hear the person out.
- Make sure you have a clear understanding of the problem.
- Be open to self-improvement and change.
- Trust that the person giving the feedback has good intentions.
- Do not react defensively.
- Don't offer excuses. If there are extenuating circumstances, specify them as facts not opinions.
- Thank the person for the feedback.
- Agree on how to move forward.

> *Praise people for what they do well, and then gradually help them with their shortcomings. This method will work well in an office, in a factory, in one's home, with spouse, children, parents, with almost anyone in the world.*
>
> Dale Carnegie

Problem Solving

Solving problems is an important part of most management jobs. Supervisors must deal with problems concerning operations, production, quality, personnel and sometimes marketing and financial areas. The most usual resource used to deal with these problems is the previous experience of the manager. If he or she has been involved in the type of work for any length of time, the chances are that similar problems have risen in the past. By applying what previously worked, there is a good possibility of resolving the problem.

Unfortunately, this does not always hold true. Sometimes a solution that had been successful in the past may not be effective this time. Although it appears to be the same problem, circumstances may be somewhat different. To avoid this, before tackling a problem, first make sure just what the problem really is.

Clarify the Problem

A major manufacturer of refrigerators had lost a significant share of its market to a competitor. In the past when market share had decreased, the reason for it was increased advertising on the part of the competitors involved, and it was overcome by increasing their own advertising. Using this past experience as a guide, they developed a good advertising campaign to overcome the current loss. To their surprise, the advertising did not help at all—in fact, the market share continued to decrease.

Further study showed that this time the competitor had not done any unusual advertising, but had increased the mark-up given to the retailers. This gave the retailer added incentive to push the competitor's product, even when the customer visited the store as a result of the new advertising. They had tackled the wrong problem. Study the problem—look for the real problem, it may not be what first appears to be.

Identify the Causes of the Problem

Often when we seek the cause of a problem, we see only the

tip of the iceberg. The problem is much deeper. We have an itchy rash, the dermatologist prescribes a salve, which we apply. The itching stops; the rash goes away. We think the problem is solved, but two weeks later it returns. What has happened? The doctor treated the symptom—the rash. True, the rash was a real problem, but it was not the real cause of the problem, which might have been an allergy or another medical situation. To find the real cause or causes of the problems in our jobs, we must look for the "critical factor(s)" from which the problem has arisen. This requires in-depth study and careful analysis.

Develop Several Possible Solutions

Typically, when faced with a problem, we may think of an immediate solution and rush it into effect. Just because a possible solution comes to mind immediately, does not mean that this is the best solution. It is far better to consider a variety of possible solutions before choosing the one to be tried.

Keep an open mind. Seek suggestions from the people who are closest to the problem—the people who work with the situation and will be involved in implementing the action that will be decided upon. Call on experts inside the company (or outside the company, if appropriate) to benefit from their experience and knowledge.

Be creative. People are more creative than they realize. By utilizing this often hidden power within us, innovative concepts can be uncovered that may solve our problems.

Determine the Best Solution

Once several alternatives have been developed, weigh all the factors and decide which is the best. To do this, it is necessary to review the problem and determine which of the solutions would be best suited to accomplish our goal.

List those items that are absolutely essential to the solution. These may include maximum cost, time limitations, use of personnel, and use of other resources. Then list those items that are not essential, but would make the chosen solution even better.

When the New Wave Hairdressers were seeking a new location, they listed the following as essential factors in making the decision:

1. The new location must be in an active shopping mall.
2. It should be no less than 4000 square feet.
3. The rent must be no more than $ "X" per month.
4. We can open for business no later than six months from now.

It would be nice if:

1. There was 4500 square feet for that rent.
2. The landlord would pay for redecorating costs.
3. There were no other hairdressers in the mall.
4. There were high fashion boutiques in the mall. These latter four are preferential factors.

New Wave would not even consider a location unless all of the essential factors are met. Then, by weighing the various preferential factors, they can determine which is the best deal for them.

Take Action

Once a decision is made, put it into effect. Each person involved in implementing the solution should be assigned his or her part, resources should be assembled and the action started. Managers should be on top of the situation. If there are some people on the staff who are not enthusiastic about the solution, "sell" it to them. Be available to help those involved to understand what has to be done, to demonstrate where appropriate, and help where needed.

Follow-Up

There are times when the type of problem requires a solution to which the company must commit itself for an extended periods (e.g., moving to a new location) of time. If the solution chosen does not work, there is little one can do to salvage it. Therefore, in such situations, the problem analysis must be performed with utmost skill. Fortunately, most problems faced by supervisors are not that permanent and can be reversed if they do not work.

When putting such a solution into effect, ask: "How long would it take to determine if this solution is working?" Then set a follow-up date accordingly. At that time, evaluate what has occurred so far and if it has not solved the problem, drop it and select one of the other alternatives. There is no reason to stick with a solution that is not effective when there are other alternatives available.

Customer Complaints

Until a perfect product, organization or company is invented, we would necessarily have to deal with negative issues from our customers. It is inevitable that problems will arise, and just as certain is the fact that some people who complain would be hard to please.

In addition to applying the principles discussed earlier in this chapter, we can effectively resolve complaints, build relationships, improve customer loyalty and retention by using the following eight-step process:

1. *Greet.* Always answer the phone or greet people in person as though you are happy to hear from them. Begin in a friendly way. This is easy to say, but can be difficult to do. We need to be able to "live in day-tight compartments" and separate any negative experiences from this customer contact. Even when the customer is a constant complainer, deal only with the current issue.

2. *Listen.* We often get the same kinds of complaints, so it becomes challenging to really listen to people. Give them an opportunity to vent some of their frustration. Be empathetic. Listen not only for facts, but also for feelings. Resist the temptation to start responding too quickly. Show that we are actively listening by brief interjections or repetition or by rephrasing the customer's comments.

3. *Ask Questions.* Ask questions to clarify the concern. It is important to recognize the need to resist responding until we understand exactly what issues the customer is concerned about.

Elementary questions capture the basic facts of the problem. This gives us an opportunity to take some of the emotion out of the complaint. For example: "When did this problem develop?"

Elaborative questions gather more details. This gives the customer a chance to expand on their feelings. These questions should be relatively short to encourage the customer to talk more. For example: "Tell me exactly what went wrong?"

Evaluative questions help us gain an understanding of the severity of the issue in the mind of the customer. For example: "What would you like us to do?" This is where we evaluate what steps we should take to satisfy the customer.

4. *Empathize.* Find a point of agreement with the person. This does not necessarily mean that you agree with the customer's complaint. This is where you show the customer that you heard and understood the concern and that you recognize its importance to them.

5. *Address the issue.* Now that the emotional issues have been addressed, you should do everything in your power to resolve the practical aspects of the complaint. You must take responsibility for the actions of your organization. If you need help to get back to the customer, do so quickly and thoroughly. This is your opportunity to turn a lemon into lemonade. People who have their problems successfully resolved tend to continue to do business with the same organization.

6. *Test questions.* Ask questions to test how well you have resolved the emotional and practical sides of the complaint. Give the customer another opportunity to talk.

7. *Offer additional help.* Ask what else you can do for this customer. This allows an opportunity to turn the conversation away from the complaint, which makes it easier to end on a positive note.

8. *Follow through.* Often complaints cannot be resolved completely during the first point of contact. Even if the complaint has been resolved, create a reason to contact the

customer again. For example, find a way to give added value. Also, look for ways to solve the root causes of problems within your organization.

Dealing with Negative Thinkers

In almost every organization, we will find people who are hostile about any new suggestions. Whenever we are for something, they're against it. They always have a reason that what we want to accomplish just can't be done.

The reasons for this negativity vary. It may stem from some real or perceived past mistreatment by the company. If that's the case, look into the matter. If the person has justifiable reasons for being negative, try to persuade them that the past is past and motivate them to look to the future. If misconceptions are involved, try to clear them up.

Negativity is often rooted in long-term personality factors that are beyond the ability of any manager to overcome. In that case, professional help is necessary.

Stop! Look! Listen!

A good rule in dealing with negative people is to acknowledge their arguments and persuade them to work with you to overcome their perceived problems, so that the project can move along. Make the person part of the solution rather than an additional problem.

Let's look at some of the problems negative people cause:

Resistance to change. Even people with a positive attitude are reluctant to change. It's comfortable to keep doing things the way they've always been done. Positive thinking people can be persuaded to change by presenting logical arguments. Negative people resist change just for the sake of resisting. No argument ever helps. They often do everything they can to sabotage a situation so that the new methods won't work and they can say, "I told you so."

Impact on group morale. Just as one rotten apple can spoil a whole barrel, one negative person can destroy the entire team's morale. Because the negativism that spreads from one person to another, it's tough to maintain team spirit under these circumstances.

When we present new ideas to negative people, get them to express their objections openly. Say something like this: "You have brought up some good points, and I appreciate them. As we move into this new program, let's carefully watch for those problems. However, we must give this new concept a try. Work with me on it, and together we'll iron out the kinks."

Negative Personalities

Anita exudes negativity. It's not what she says—it's how she acts. She takes any suggestion as a personal affront and takes on any new assignment with such reluctance and annoyance that she turns everyone off.

People such as Anita often don't realize how they come across to others. They probably act this way in their personal lives as well as on their jobs. They're the type of people who don't get along with their families, have few friends, and are forever the dissenters. A good start in dealing with such people is to have a heart-to-heart talk with them to let them know how their attitude affects your group's morale. Surprisingly, many negative thinking people have no idea that their behavior is disruptive to others.

Suggest that they enroll in a personal improvement program, such as the Dale Carnegie Course. Such programs have helped many people overcome negativity, resulting in not only improvement in their job performance, but their entire lives.

Work Towards a Win-Win Situation

If everybody isn't winning—nobody is truly winning. Creating "losers" ultimately results in lost customers, employee turnover, antagonistic work groups, and companies operating below potential.

By careful preparation and by keeping in mind the best techniques of dealing with people, we can present and sell our ideas to others and gain the great satisfaction of seeing our ideas carried out with enthusiasm by everyone involved.

Sum and Substance

There is no better summary of getting the best of an argument, whether it is with family members, social acquaintances, or on the job than Dale Carnegie's principles on persuading others to accept our ideas. They are:

1. Show respect for the other person's opinion. Never tell a person he or she is wrong.
2. If you are wrong, admit it quickly, emphatically.
3. Begin in a friendly way.
4. Get the other person to say, "yes" immediately.
5. Let the other person do a great deal of the talking.

6. Let the other person feel the idea is his or hers.
7. Try honestly to see things from the other person's point of view.
8. Be sympathetic with the other person's ideas and desires.
9. Appeal to the nobler motives.
10. Dramatize your ideas.
11. Throw down a challenge.

7

MAKING MEETINGS MORE MEANINGFUL

A frequently used and effective communication technique is meetings. It enables the communication to be delivered to a large group of people at the same time. But meetings can be a big waste of time if they're not organized properly.

In most businesses and organizations a good deal of work is assigned to committees. There's an old joke that says that a camel is a horse created by a committee. As long as there have been committees, they have had a reputation of not really being effective. Yet, often old aphorisms provide conflicting messages. Are committees made up of "too many cooks who spoil the broth," or do they benefit because "two heads are better than one?" Let's look at what can be done to make the committees on which *we* serve accomplish the mission for which they were created.

Establish Clear and Understandable Goals

When Leonard B. was appointed to chair a committee consisting of three other executives and himself to find a suitable location for a branch warehouse, he called a meeting to set specific goals and timetables. Rather than dictating these to his people, he conducted a participative planning session. Each of the members contributed ideas and together they came up with a workable plan. Because each of the committee members was involved in the planning, the goals were not only clear to each of them, but the entire group was committed to its accomplishment.

Every member of the committee should be given a specific assignment. The chairperson should learn the strengths and specific areas of expertize of each of the members and utilize these assets in making the assignments. Leonard had the advantage of knowing each of his team members as they had worked together for some time and was able to assign each of them meaningful assignments pertaining to areas where they could contribute most effectively.

However, if you chair a committee where some or all of the members are virtual strangers, learn as early as possible about each of them. When Carol was appointed to chair a PTA committee to study and make recommendations on the development of a program for more participation in classroom activities, she had only a casual acquaintance with most of the members. She made a point to meet each of them privately over the first few weeks to find out where they could do the most good. At the second meeting, she was not only able to make wise appointments, but as a result of these personal discussions, encouraged many of them to volunteer to take on significant aspects of the project.

Once the assignment is made, ask each of the committee members to develop a plan and a timetable for his or her assignment. These should be put in writing and submitted to the chairperson at the next meeting. To assure that the plan is being met, a follow-up system should be established.

Leonard's committee's goal was to find the location and arrange for the leasing of the facility within three months. So each of his members had to have the plans for his or her assignment ready two weeks from the first meeting. Follow-up discussions with each of the members were scheduled during the two week period after the second meeting and a third full committee meeting was scheduled at the beginning of the second month.

Carol's project was much longer. Her committee had a six-month deadline. Inasmuch as Carol's group consisted of nine people, she created three sub-committees for the three major aspects of the project and arranged to meet with each sub-committee once during the first and second month. Monthly meetings were scheduled for the entire committee to report and to share their ideas and accomplishments.

Resolving Disagreements

Whenever several people are involved in a project, there is likely to be some disagreements. It is the responsibility of the chairperson to resolve them. Carol faced this at her first meeting with a sub-committee. Two of the members agreed on a plan of action, but the third member firmly opposed it. Logically, a two to one vote might be used to choose the plan, but Carol recognized that it was necessary to win the full cooperation of the third member if the plan was to succeed.

She asked the dissenter to express her reasons for opposing the majority and listened carefully. She encouraged the others to think about these objections and together they were able to reach a consensus and develop a plan to which all of them could commit themselves. Some suggestions on how to deal with disagreements will be discussed later in this chapter.

Committee Reports

Once each of the members or sub-committees has completed the assigned work, the results are presented to the entire committee. These are discussed and final decisions or recommendations are made. Usually, a full report must be developed for submission to the person or persons to whom the committee is responsible. In most committees this is the end of the assignment. However, in some cases the committee may be responsible for implementing the action recommended.

Carol's committee had to submit a detailed report to the PTA Board. Inasmuch as each of her sub-committees had investigated a different aspect of the subject, she asked for written reports from each of them. After they had been discussed in the entire committee and decisions were made, the sub-committee revised their reports to reflect these decisions. Carol appointed one of the members to write the draft of the committee report. This was carefully reviewed and edited and copies sent to each of the committee members. At the final meeting of the committee, the report was approved.

Leonard's committee worked somewhat differently. Each of the members had been given a different aspect of the assignment. One member had studied traffic patterns; another cost factors and the third community desirability. Once this specialized information was obtained, several meetings were held to discuss the entire problem. From these a final recommendation and report was written. All the members contributed to the report and it was put into final shape by the chairperson. But this was not the end of the assignment. After the written report was submitted, Leonard had to meet his bosses to answer questions and defend some of the recommendations. Knowing that this was usual in these circumstances, the committee planned for the oral presentation and for questions or objections that might be raised. As a result Leonard was fully prepared to make a full presentation, answer questions, and rebut objections.

Successful committee work requires careful planning, assigning each of the aspects of the work to people who are competent, getting all of the members involved, and following up to assure that what is planned and assigned is carried out effectively. When you get each member to participate from the planning stage to the final report, the work of the group would go smoothly and the mission of the committee will be effectively accomplished.

Making Committees Work

We have often heard committee members complain: "What a waste of time. I could have accomplished so much more if I had spent this past hour at my desk!" In a recent survey, over 70 percent of the people interviewed felt they had wasted time in the meetings they had attended.

There is hope. Meetings can be made productive. Let's look at a few ways to conduct meetings more efficiently.

Limit Who Attends

Invite only appropriate participants. Some managers hold staff meetings on a regular basis—sometimes weekly or even daily. Quite often, many of the people who attend are not involved in the matters that are being discussed. By inviting only those who can contribute to the meeting or would be affected by what is being discussed, we can avoid wasting others' time and keep the meetings briefer.

When people who are usually invited to meetings are not invited, they may worry: "Why wasn't I asked? Is the boss giving me a hidden message? Am I on the way out?" Avoid this concern by explaining beforehand the new policy and why it is being instituted.

Plan an Agenda—and Stick To It

An agenda is the key to success or failure of a meeting. Plan the agenda carefully, covering all matters that are to be discussed. By determining in advance not only what subjects will be addressed, but the order in which they would be covered, the meeting will run more smoothly.

In establishing the sequence of topics at a meeting, put the most complex ones at the beginning of the program. People come to meetings with clear minds and are able to approach deeper matters more effectively early on. If the important issues are scheduled for later consideration, participants are less likely to be attentive, and might be distracted by what has been discussed earlier.

At least three days before the meeting, the agenda should be sent to all those people who are supposed to attend the meeting. This will allow them to study the topics of discussion and prepare their contribution.

Stick rigidly to the agenda. Topics not on the agenda should not be introduced unless it's an emergency. In that case, it to be placed on the agenda for the next meeting.

Get Everyone Into the Act

Attendees should be encouraged to study the agenda and be prepared to discuss each item. If specific data is needed to make a point, organize it into easy-to-follow visuals (for example, charts or hand-outs) and bring it to the meeting. Encourage discussion and create an atmosphere in which people can disagree without fear of ridicule or retaliation.

If pertinent, provide "takeaway" photocopies of diagrams, flow charts or other visuals that were projected. Distribute the copies to everyone at the meeting to ensure that they have a clear idea of the subjects discussed. These copies also serve as permanent reminders of the material; participants can refer to them later if necessary.

If there are heftier handouts or other dense reading materials, distribute them far enough in advance of the meeting to enable team members to study them. The focus of a meeting should be on expanding, demonstrating, and clarifying information—not to introduce brand new concepts, particularly complex technical material.

As the leader of the meeting, ask questions that stimulates discussion. Be open to questions and dissension. It's better to have people butt heads during the meeting than let them stew over their problems over a long period of time.

Don't Dominate the Meeting

Gus J. prided himself in running meetings. He boasted about how all his people contributed to the subjects discussed. His staff, however, had an entirely different perception of those meetings. "Gus tells us what he plans to do, then asks if we have any ideas. When one of us suggests something, he immediately rejects it, sometimes ridiculing the person who made the suggestion. So generally, we all agree. There is no real participation."

> *This is a hurried age we are living in. If you've got anything to say, say it quickly, get to the point and stop, and give the other person a chance to talk.*
>
> *Dale Carnegie*

Control Chatterboxes

Brad is one of those people who try to dominate a meeting. He always has something to say—usually not important, often a personal pet peeve which is always distracting.

Here are some tips on how leaders can attempt to keep Brad and others like him quiet:

> Take Brad aside before the meeting and tell him, "I know you like to contribute to our meetings and I appreciate it, but we have a limited amount of time and some of the other people want a chance to present their ideas. So let's give them a chance to talk, and you and I can discuss our issues after the meeting."

> If Brad still insists on dominating the meeting, wait until he pauses for a breath—which he inevitably must do—and

quickly say: "Thank you, Brad, now let's hear what Sue has to say."

> Announce that each speaker has only three minutes to make his or her point. Be flexible with others, but be strict with blabbermouths like Brad.

Close With a Bang

At the end of the meeting, after all the items on the agenda have been covered, the leader should summarize what has been accomplished. If team member received an assignment during the course of the meeting, have them indicate what did they understand with respect to the expectation and the course of action. This will give the leader and all the participants a feedback.

Take Notes

Take notes or assign a participant to take notes, so that there is no misunderstanding of what has been decided at a meeting. These need not be detailed transcripts of the entire discussion, but a summary of the decisions made on each issue. After the meeting, distribute copies of the notes not only to the attendees, but also to all the people who may be affected by what was determined. The notes would serve as a reminder to the participants of the meeting and as a communication to those who didn't attend.

Meetings in Volunteer Organizations

The same rules that apply to conducting business meetings should be applied in board meetings of volunteer organizations, such as religious groups, community associations, social clubs and similar societies. Sometimes these meetings are conducted in a more formal manner.

The usual structure of these meetings calls for starting with a reading of the notes from the previous meeting and, if necessary, making corrections on it. This may be followed by reports made by the chairs of various sub-committees, then a discussion of old business, followed by new business. An agenda covering the reports on "old business" is no problem, but there is little control over "new businesses."

Sandra was presiding over the board meeting of the Home Owners Association. It was 9 PM and they had just completed the old business section. As it was getting late, and Sandra had things to do at home, when she called for "new business," she crossed her fingers and hoped nothing would be brought up.

Sure enough, one board member had a pet project he was trying to promote, and the meeting went on for another hour.

To overcome this problem, suggest that the rules be changed. Instead of "new business," substitute, "suggestions for the next meeting." By doing this, although ideas may be introduced, no discussion can take place and the meeting will conclude much earlier. Control over the meeting is assured by sticking to the agenda. Other matters can be deferred until they can be incorporated into the agenda.

How to Disagree Without Being Disagreeable

Chairing a meeting does not always run smoothly. There are participants who disagree with you and are often adamant in their opinions. Here are some suggestions on how to deal with these people.

Accept the fact that the person disagreeing with you may

be right. You do not have all the answers. Ask questions to help understand where that person is coming from. Listen to fully understand and appreciate why this person holds that belief. Clarify any misunderstandings. He or she may not have fully understood your evidence. On the other hand, that person may have brought up some facts that you were not aware of and which may require you to reexamine your argument.

Often the reason for disagreement is emotional not factual. The person may be reacting negatively to your idea for some personal reason—perhaps a poor experience with a similar idea in the past of some facet of his or her personality. Arguing on the basis of evidence is futile. Try to determine the true reason for the disagreement and if possible, deal with it.

Do not become confrontational. Instead of saying: "You don't understand…" say: "The way I understand it …." When we blame the other person for not agreeing with us, we put them on the defensive front and incur resentment that will work against ever convincing them to accept our ideas.

Reread the suggestions on how to disagree without being disagreeable in chapter 6.

Meeting Self-Evaluator

Next time we conduct a meeting, we can review our effectiveness with the following checklist.

Before the meeting:

1. Did we prepare an agenda for the meeting?
2. Did we distribute agenda to participants in advance of meeting?

3. Did we set starting and ending times for the meeting?
4. Did we prepare visuals and/or handouts?
5. Did we assign segments of the program to participants?
6. Did we appoint a participant to record the meeting by taking notes?
7. Did we arrange for all the equipment and supplies required:
    Chalk board and chalk
    Flip chart easel
    Flip chart pads and markers
    Computer & projector for powerpoint
    Overhead projector
    Slide projector
    Other

During the meeting:

1. Did we stick to the agenda?
2. Did we manage to obtain participation from all participants?
3. Did we keep blabbermouths and dominators under control?
4. Did we distribute assignments equitably?
5. Did we refrain from expressing our ideas until participants expressed theirs?
6. Did we encourage questions from participants?
7. Did we encourage other participants to answer questions asked by team members?
8. Did we summarize key points at the end of meeting?
9. Did we verify participants' understanding of their assignments before adjourning the meeting?
10. Did we end the meeting with a motivational statement or a call for action?

After the meeting:

1. Did we distribute notes from the meeting to the participants and others who may be affected?
2. Did we follow through on assignments made?
3. Did we gather feedback from participants about the meeting?

The more "yes" answers, the more effectively the meeting was conducted.

> *Successful people will profit from their mistakes and try again in a different way.*
>
> *Dale Carnegie*

Get the Most Out of Meetings

When we lead the meeting, we have control over how well it runs, but most of the times we are not the leader but a participant. By taking active steps before, during, and after the meeting, we can make every meeting that we attend a valuable learning experience.

When you are notified of the meeting, don't just enter it on your calendar and forget it until the scheduled time. It's worth taking the time to prepare for it.

Before the meeting:

➤ Study the agenda. Review the subjects that are listed. Even if you have enough knowledge about them, you should make sure that you are up to date on them. Review your files to find out know what's been done so far. If pertinent, read articles in technical or trade publications that cover the matters.

- If it is a new area or one with which you are not familiar with, carefully study the material provided. This is too important to just give it a cursory scan and expect to pick up the details at the meeting.
- Make notes on comments, ideas, or questions that you have about the subjects.

At the meeting:

- Participate: If you have comments, ideas, or questions, don't hold back. Caution: Don't just talk for the sake of talking. Make your points succinctly.
- Deal with disagreements. It's likely that some other participants may disagree with your view. Don't take it personally. In responding, stick to the facts. It's a discussion, not an argument.
- Work toward consensus. If the objective of the meeting is to solve a problem, contribute toward the solution. Listen to other views. They may be better than yours. Be ready to make compromises to attain satisfactory solutions.
- Don't dominate the meeting. Sometimes it's hard to hold back when you have ideas that you want to express. Give the others a chance to talk.
- Take notes on key decisions that were made, or on new information that you have learned.
- If assignments are to given to the participants, volunteer immediately for the assignment that most appeals to you. If you hold back, you may wind up with a job that is not as interesting and which you may not enjoy doing.

After the meeting:

Review your notes. Take action where required. If you were given an assignment, discuss it with the leader to assure you understood what is required and when it is expected.

Attending Meetings Outside

Many people attend meetings outside of the company. They may be seminars, trade association meetings or conventions, or conferences sponsored by organizations that have ideas or proposals that may be of interest to our company or us. These may be held within the company or outside the company's premises.

Here are some suggestions to help us make these meetings worth our time and attention.

Prepare for the meeting

Most conferences and conventions are announced months in advance. Prepare for this meeting in the same way as you would have for a company meeting. Usually an agenda accompanies the announcement. Study it carefully. Does any subject listed require special preparation? You may want to read up on unfamiliar subjects to help yourself comprehend and contribute to the discussion. You may want to re-examine your company's experience in that area so you could relate what is being discussed to your own organization's problems.

Meet new people

At the meeting, don't sit with your colleagues. You can speak to them any time. If attendees are seated at a table, make a point of sitting with different people at various stages of the meetings. Often at luncheon or dinner discussions, you pick up more ideas from your tablemates than from the speakers. Note the names and addresses of people you meet at these events. They may be a source of information or guidance in the future

When speakers from outside address a meeting, note their names and addresses. You may want to contact some of them for more information.

Keep an open mind

To get the most out of what a speaker says, keep your mind open to new suggestions. They may be different from what you honestly believe is best, but until you hear it all and think it through objectively, you wouldn't really know. Progress comes through change. This does not mean that all new ideas are good ones, but they should be heard out, evaluated and carefully and objectively considered.

Be tolerant

Sometimes you hear a speaker who immediately turned you off. You didn't like his or her appearance, clothes, voice, or regional accent so you either stopped listening or rejected what he or she said. Prejudice against a speaker keeps many attendees from really listening to what is being discussed or from accepting the ideas being presented.

Take notes

Note taking has two important functions: It helps organize what you hear while you are at the meeting, resulting in, systematic listening; it also becomes a source for future reference.

Keep an Ah Hah! page

Use this page in your notebook to list exciting ideas that you pick up at the meeting. These are items that you want to make sure you don't forget.

Ask questions

Don't hesitate to question a speaker when the opportunity arises. But don't waste time asking trivial questions. Avoid prefacing your question with lengthy comments. Be clear; be brief.

During a formal presentation, it is not appropriate to interrupt the speaker. If you have a question, jot it down on the last page of your notebook. This should act as a reminder to not to forget the questions that you want to ask when the opportune time comes.

Be an active participant

Contribute ideas. In most meetings there are people who willingly share ideas and information. Others just sit and listen. When asked why they did not participate fully, a commonly heard response is: "Why should I give my ideas to these people? Some of them are my competitors and I won't give away my trade secrets."

Nobody expects us to say anything that would damage our firm or its competitive position, but most discussions are not of this nature. They're designed to promote the exchange of ideas that are of value to most of the attendees. The experience of one organization helps the others. By contributing ideas, we provide richer experiences for others, which in turn results in a more fulfilling experience for ourselves.

After the meeting:

After the meeting, summarize what you learned. Review our notes while the meeting is still fresh in your mind. As soon as possible, write or dictate a report on the conference for the creation of a permanent file.

Report on what you have learned. Send a memo or brief report to your boss and your colleagues, who might find the information valuable. By sharing what you have learned, you add to the value of your firm and yourself, for attending the program.

Put it into practice

If nothing is done with what you learned at the meeting, it's has been a waste of time and money. Therefore, put what you have learned into practice.

Sum and Substance

> Every meeting should have a purpose, and the meeting's leader should make sure the purpose is accomplished.
> Several days before the meeting, prepare an agenda and distribute it to everybody who is expected at the meeting.
> Prepare materials and arrange for equipments intended to be used in advance and make sure the equipment required to show visuals is on hand. Make sure that there are enough copies of handouts for all participants.
> Establish a participative climate, facilitate participation by shy or reticent participants, and encourage all attendees to participate. Don't allow blabbermouths to dominate the meeting.

- By the time the meeting ends, participants should be clear about the subjects discussed. Give everyone a chance to ask questions and summarize what has been accomplished. Assure that if any participants received assignments during the meeting, they have understood what they are supposed to do and when to do it. End the meeting with a call for action or an inspirational message.
- We can get the most out of meetings or conferences we attend by following the suggestions made in the last section of this chapter.

8

PUT IT IN WRITING

"When I talk to somebody in person or on the telephone, I have no trouble making myself understood, but when I have to write a letter or a memo, I sound stilted and inadequate." This comment was not made by a high school dropout, but a graduate engineer with a master's degree in business administration. Many people who are articulate in oral communications freeze up when conveying their ideas on paper.

Part of the reason that this occurs is the mistaken notion that written words should sound more formal than the spoken message. This results in letters and memos that sound stiff and artificial.

Written words differ from spoken words because the meaning conveyed by oral communication is tempered by voice tone and body language. In addition, if the meaning is not clear, the speaker knows this immediately by the manner in which the message is received and the questions asked by the other party.

Some men and woman try to avoid a project that requires a written report. They feel inadequate and ill prepared to take on this assignment. There is no more reason to fear a written report than to give an oral report. It is a learnable skill and when mastered can enhance a person's career growth.

People who accept responsibility make themselves stand out from the others in the office, factory or in any walk of life, and they are the ones who get ahead. Welcome responsibility. Do this in little things and in big things and success will come to you.

—Dale Carnegie

In order to make sure that the written message comes across to the reader with the same impact as spoken words, the language of our letters and memos must be somewhat different from the language used in speaking. Yet, it need not be too different. The following suggestions will help you write in much the same way as you speak without sounding stilted.

Plan the Message Before Writing One Word

Think before writing. Deborah K. has received many compliments about her letters. She rightfully prides herself on this. Deborah outlines each letter carefully before dictating or writing it.

A study of Deborah's outlines indicate that she does not only list points to be covered, but puts them in order of importance so the letter immediately starts with what is of most interest to the correspondent. Rather than leading up to the critical information with background material, she states it immediately and follows it up with additional matters that are absolutely necessary to make the point.

For example, instead of the common beginning: "We are in receipt of your letter requesting information about our Model #1754, and so on," she writes: "Yes, our Model #1754 will solve your problem," and then provides evidence. Instead of ending: "Thank you for your inquiry," she concluded with: "We look forward to receiving your order." Statements such as these indicate a direct and dynamic response to the inquiry and precipitate immediate positive action.

TAB the Message

A good rule to follow is to carefully plan what we want to say before writing a single word. This simple process will help plan the letter or memo. It can be summarized in the acronym TAB, which provides clues to help us think clearly about what we want to write before writing it.

Think about the situation: Why am I writing this?
Action: What do I want to accomplish?
Benefit: How will this be of value to the reader?

Ask these questions and jot down the answers on a scratch pad. By "TAB-ing" our thoughts before we do the writing, we get a clear idea of what we want to convey. The list will help us organize all the information concerning the situation we're writing about—it will indicate what we want to accomplish, how to deal with it, and how those actions would benefit our readers.

Be Complete, Concise, and Clear

How can a letter be kept concise and still be complete and clear? Many writers include much extraneous material in a letter or memo. When Enrique returned from a business trip to Latin America, his report was ten pages long. It certainly was complete, but much of what he wrote was incidental information that had no bearing on his mission. He reported everything he saw and heard rather than concentrating on the objectives of his trip.

Ask these questions before writing a long letter or report: "What are the key matters to be discussed?"

"How can I present these matters in the most concise form and provide all the information as clearly as possible?"

After writing the first draft, reread each sentence and ask: "Is this sentence really needed?"

Avoid Jargon

The letter he was reading puzzled Gary. The writer kept referring to the advantages of dealing with an "OEM" and Gary had no idea what those letters meant. The writer incorrectly assumed that Gary knew they meant Original Equipment Manufacturer,' and by making this false assumption, failed to convey the message. Initials, acronyms and other jargon have a place when communicating with people in the fields where that jargon is used. One cannot assume that others will know these terms.

However, in writing a letter using the jargon of the field in which the recipient of the letter works, may result in an acceptance by the reader.

Use Short, Punchy Sentences

We may be impressed by our own excellent rhetoric, but the reader of our letter will find it much more understandable if we avoid complex, multi-phrase sentences. The simple declarative sentence is often the best. Instead of saying: "In light of the research in this field, it is our opinion that the program we are offering will facilitate the writing skills of the employees who undertake this training," say: "This program will teach your people to write better."

However, avoid structuring all sentences in the same manner. This will make the letter boring. Short and punchy—yes; simple and dull—no. Make the main points in capsule form like the headline of a newspaper story; supplement them with details where appropriate by using more varied word structure.

Get to the Point

Steer clear of complex sentence constructions or extravagant phraseology. Keep it as brief as possible, but make it punchy. One way of making points stand out is to write the item in the form of a bulletin:

- Headline the main point—use bold print.
- Break the body of the letter or memo into separate sections, one for each subsidiary point.
- Use an asterisk (*) or bullet (•) to highlight key points.
- Where appropriate, use graphs, charts, or other visual aids to augment the impact of your words.

Talk to the Reader

The message will be clearer and more easily accepted by the reader if it is written in the way we speak. Pretend the person who is going to read the letter or report is sitting in your office, or you are on the telephone with them. Be informal. Relax. Talk in the manner—the vocabulary, accents, idioms and expressions—which you usually use.

We wouldn't normally say: "Please be advised ..." or "We wish to inform you that because of the fire in our plant, there will be a ten day delay in shipping your order." Instead we would get right into the message: "Because of the fire in our plant, there will be a ten day delay in shipping your order." So why not write just that?

Use Direct Questions

A conversation is not one sided. One person speaks, and then the other responds, often with a question. "Yes, but how will this affect the quality?" By interjecting questions in the letter, we can draw the attention of the reader to specific points. After making a point, ask a pertinent question such as: "What additional applications can you find by installing this software?" This gives the reader a chance to reflect on your message in terms that are specific to his or her needs.

Write Like You Speak

When speaking we use *I*, *we* and *you* all the time. They're part of the normal give and take of our conversation. In writing we tend to be more formal. We use phrases like "It is assumed," "it is recommended," or sentences like: "An investigation will be made and upon its completion a report will be furnished to your organization." Why not clearly state: "We're investigating the matter and when we obtain the information we'll let you know."

Make the letter sound more personal. Use the addressee's name within the letter. If they are friends, we may use the first name, if business acquaintances, use the appropriate title (Mr., Mrs., Ms., Dr., etc.), and the last name, and instead of saying "the company will benefit by using this product," say "So you see, Beth, (or Ms. Smith), how using this product will benefit you."

Use Short, Snappy Sentences

The ordinary reader can take in only so many words before his or her eyes come to a brief rest at a period. If a sentence has too many words, chances are that the full meaning would be missed. Studies show that sentences of no more than 20 words are easiest to read and absorb. It is usually quite clear to see where one idea leaves off and another begins. Limit each sentence to one idea. Remember your objective is to get the idea across to the reader—not to create undying prose. It is also helpful to use short rather than long words.

Of course, technical language is appropriate while writing on technical matters to technically trained people. However, when writing to people who may not have the background in your area, avoid language and jargon that they are unlikely to possess.

Give Letters the Right Human Touch

Expressing our natural feelings personalizes the message. If it's good news, say you're glad; if it's bad news, say you're sorry. You should be as courteous, polite and interested as if the addressee is in front of you. Remember the person who is going to read the letter is a human being, they would be annoyed if the letter is cold and pleased if it is courteous and friendly.

Make Mail and Memos Memorable

Memos and letters are in a sense "visual," but when we read them, it becomes an audio input. We absorb the data by reading them to ourselves. The mind processes this in the same way that it deals with words that it hears. By augmenting memos and letters with visual aids, those documents become far more effective. Most people prefer to study a graph or chart than read a column of figures. By taking a little more time to convert information into graphic format, memos and reports could have much greater impact. For people who like to read figures, they can be included as back-up data. If drawings, photographs or other visual images can be used, the memo becomes a simulcast.

There are many computer programs available that can easily convert data into a variety of graphs and charts. And, if these charts are presented in color, the impact is enhanced. Where graphics are not applicable, use word pictures in the memos. Let's look at two memos about labor turnover:

"The turnover in the Shipping Department has caused a heavy workload for the shipping personnel, resulting in accidents, illness due to fatigue, and more resignations. This has led to orders not being shipped and customer complaints."

Now let's use some word pictures: "I walked into the shipping department this morning. Only six people were working instead of the full staff of ten. They were working under tremendous pressure trying to get the orders out. They had put in ten hours yesterday and I could see the fatigue in their faces and in the way they worked. One man was limping as a result of a minor accident. While I was there, three customers called complaining about not getting their orders when promised."

The first memo told the facts, but the second example allowed the reader of that memo to "see" the situation. By using visuals and word pictures where appropriate, communications—both oral and written—can become clearer and more dramatic.

Watch Grammar and Spelling

We can't always depend on a secretary to correct our grammar, sentence structure, and spelling errors. Today, many managers don't have secretaries or administrative assistants. They write their own correspondence. If you are weak in grammar or spelling, seek out a colleague to be your in-company "editor" for constructive review and suggestions. The "spell-check" feature in a word-processing program is a great help, as it catches most typos and misspellings, but you still must reread the document carefully. It can't catch all of them. Even if you are one of the lucky few who has an assistant, you should still check everything that goes out with your signature on it.

Ending the Letter

Before writing the final paragraph of a letter or memo, review what it is that you wish to accomplish. If the letter is a response to a request for information, did you provide the information requested? If the letter is intended to obtain action from the recipient, have you specified what action you demand?

Keep in mind that the final paragraph is your last chance to make your point. Just as a good salesperson always ends a sales call or sales letter by asking for the order, any good letter writer should ask at the end of the letter that the recipient take the action that the letter has addressed. A thank you is always appropriate, but by itself it is not enough. Instead of saying: "Thank you for your consideration," it is far better to end the letter with: "Thank you for signing and returning the enclosed maintenance agreement, which will assure you of worry-free use of your equipment for the next twelve months."

Letter writing can be improved by planning your letters and following the above suggestions to make each letter present your message in an easy-to-read, yet forceful style.

Dealing with Incoming Correspondence

As noted earlier in this book, communication is a two-way street. We not only send information, but also receive information. We learned how to be effective receivers of oral communication in previous chapters. How we receive written communications is also important.

Reading and responding to letters and memos can take an inordinate amount of time and energy.

Every morning, when Don M. emptied his in-basket, he would read each of the letters, memos, brochures and other items and carefully divide them into four neatly stacked piles. In the first pile, he placed letters and memos that required immediate response; in the second pile, those for which he needed additional information or could delegate to a subordinate; the third for materials on which he didn't have to take any action, just read them and file them away and the fourth was the junk mail that would be immediately discarded.

He scheduled a time for responding to his correspondences at a convenient time each day. At that time, he would reread each letter so he could respond appropriately. At another time during the day, he would reread the memos and letters in the second pile, obtain the required information or delegate it to somebody else. As he had already read the memos and letters in the third pile—those that did not require any action on his part, they were given to his secretary to be filed.

The time involved in reading and rereading each of those pieces of correspondence took an inordinate amount of Don's working day. We can deal with this much more effectively by following certain ideas:

Read a letter or memo once and take immediate action

When you read a letter the first time, make notes on a Post-It slip on the key points that would require a response. Then when you dictate or write your reply, it is not necessary to reread the entire letter. It may only save two or three minutes per letter, but if you respond to 30 letters a day, this saves 90 minutes that can be used on more productive matters.

Use the same approach with letters or memos for which you need additional information. During the first reading, note what information is needed, the source from which it can be obtained, to whom it should be delegated and any pertinent instructions.

Don't answer a memo with another memo

We receive a memo from the manager of another department asking for the current inventory of a list of items, specifying the items by name and stock number. Typically, we respond by writing a memo stating: "As per your request, here is the current inventory of the following items." Then we list each of the items by name and stock number and the quantity on hand.

It's more effective to just write the quantities next to the item name and number on the original memo. This saves considerable time and serves the purpose. In many cases copies are not even needed, but if there is a need, make a photocopy of the original memo with the noted data. A similar approach can be taken in replying to letters from outside the organization. If the inquiry made by the correspondent can be answered by a single sentence, just write the reply on the bottom of the letter received and send it back to the sender.

However, if it is company policy to answer correspondence in a more formal way, take the time to write a letter. Sometimes the image we present to our customers or the public is more important than time saved.

Delegate correspondence

Often the information requested in a letter or memo must be obtained from a subordinate. Instead of asking the subordinate to just obtain the information, give that person the full responsibility of writing the reply. This not only saves time, but gives the subordinate valuable experience in performing the entire task. In the beginning you would probably want to read and sign the final letter, but once the subordinate becomes more and more familiar with the areas covered, it may not be necessary for you to become involved at all.

Dump it

Many letters and memos are sent by other departments just to familiarize us to their contents and does not require any action. It is unlikely that we will ever need to see them again. Don't file them—just dump them! This may be a shocking thing to do in many companies, but there is no real need to save most of these memos. If in a remote situation a discarded file is needed, the person who wrote it and the person who received the original undoubtedly can provide us with a copy. Dumping letters and memos on which no action is required does not only save us time, but it saves considerable time for our clerical staff and keeps those file cabinets from becoming overstuffed.

The Email Explosion

As much attention to writing emails should be given as we do to the composition of standard letters and memos. Remember that email is a form of written communication. Many people think of it as a substitute for a phone call rather than a letter, so they dash off their messages with little or no consideration of style or even content. Unlike the phone call, email can be kept either electronically or as a printout, so it should be carefully planned and composed.

More and more inter and intra-office communications are now done via email. According to a poll conducted by Ernst & Young, 36 percent of respondents use email more than any other communication tool, including the telephone.

Today many managers, particularly the younger generation, use text messaging, sometimes called SMS (Short Message Service) with their mobile communication devices in addition to or instead of emails. The use of text messaging for business purposes has grown significantly during the first decade of the

21st century. Some practical uses of text messaging include the use of SMS for sending alerts (e.g. "The phone system is down"), for confirming delivery or other tasks, and for instant communication between a service provider and a client (e.g. stock broker and investor).

To use text messaging when sending more detailed information, follow the same suggestions presented here for sending effective emails.

Make Email Exciting, Expressive, and Engaging

Here are some tips to help write better emails and text messages:

> Think carefully about what needs to be written. If the message is more than just casual chitchat, plan it as carefully as a formal letter. If we're giving instructions, make sure the reader knows just exactly what action we're requesting. If we're answering an inquiry, make sure we've gathered all the information necessary to respond appropriately to the questions asked.

> Use a meaningful subject line. Our correspondent may receive dozens, even hundreds, of email messages each day. To ensure that our message will be read promptly, use a subject heading that will be meaningful to the addressee. For example, instead of "re your email of 6/25," use the subject line to refer to the information contained in the email (for instance, "Sales figures for June").

> Follow the suggestions given earlier in this chapter on writing letters and memos. Use the TAB approach. Use short, punchy sentences. Be clear, concise and complete. Keep to the point and be brief.

> If files are attached to the email, specify in the text which

files are attached, so the reader can check to make sure they all came through.

> Do not use abbreviations, jargon or short cuts unless you are sure the receiver understands them.

> Read the message carefully and spell-check it before clicking "Send now." If not satisfied, don't send it. Postpone the transmission. Review it, and then rewrite it. Make sure it's okay before it is sent.

If you believe in what you are doing, then let nothing hold you up in your work. Much of the best work in the world has been done against seeming impossibilities. The point is to get the work done.

Dale Carnegie

Email Clutter

Some people are so bogged down with email, they have no time to read it and still get other work done.

In many companies, employees spend an inordinate amount of time on the computer emailing jokes, personal messages, offerings ("I have six cute kittens looking for a home"), and information that is usually unimportant to most recipients. Some companies alleviate such clutter, or SPAM, in their regular email by setting up a special "classified ad" or bulletin board email address for these messages.

Another example of clutter is sending an email to an entire mailing list when only a few people on the list need the information. For example, some people, planning to take a day off, announce their plans to the "Everyone" list, thereby alerting 35 people, what only five or six people really need to know. Perhaps, they do so to puff up their own sense of self-importance, or more likely, they find it easier to send a message to everyone than to figure out who really needs to know and just click on those names. In replying to an email, don't click "reply all" unless *all* the recipients need to know the reply.

Email glut can result in the message being ignored or inadvertently deleted. Ask the receiver to acknowledge receipt of the email. If the matters involved are very important, follow up with a telephone call to ensure that the message was received and understood.

"Who's Reading my Emails?"

How private is our email? Not very. Sure, we may have a password and assume that it ensures privacy, but hackers have shown that they can easily break through even sophisticated systems. Assume anything we email can be intercepted. If confidentiality is required, email is not the medium to use.

Remember that any email sent via the company computer can be read by anybody in the company. Over the past few years there have been cases in which employees were fired because of emails they sent that violated company rules. The courts threw out their employees' claims of invasion of privacy.

More serious are the cases of people who have made comments or jokes in their email that were considered sexually or racially harassing. Printouts of such email have been entered as evidence in suits against employees' companies, even though company officials weren't aware of the messages. This has led to termination of the senders, as well as legal action against both the senders and the companies.

Email Versus Phone Calls or Visits

Many people tend to resort to email rather than make a phone call or a personal visit. Using email is often an easy way out. We don't have to leave our desks, and it's less time consuming than a telephone call. There's no time wasted in small talks or lengthy discussion about a project. All that's sent is the basic message. But often, that small talk and discussion on pros-and-cons is important. In addition, the phone call allows for instant feedback. It not only helps clarify the message, but it ensures that we and the other person both understand the matters involved in the same way.

Don't replace phone and personal contacts with email. Voice-to-voice or face-to-face contact with people with whom we deal with on a regular basis strengthens the personal relationship that is so important in building and maintaining rapport.

Summary of Email Dos and Don'ts

1. Do carefully plan emails and text messages.
2. Do read and re-read the message before clicking "send now."
3. Do inform recipients when the email doesn't require a reply. It will save both parties time and clutter.
4. Do use bullets instead of paragraphs. It makes it easier to read and grasp key points.
5. Do respond promptly to emails received, especially when immediate attention is required. Speed of communication is the chief advantage of this medium.
6. Don't send off-color jokes or stories on company email.

7. Do check whether an important email has been received by asking the respondent to acknowledge it and/or by following-up with a phone call.

8. Don't play games, or send or respond to chain letters or waste time on similar things on company time and on company computers.

9. Don't download pornographic material or items that are derogatory to any racial or ethnic groups on company computers. Remember that your emails can be read by anybody and may offend other people in the organization. It could lead to embarrassment and possibly charges of sexual or racial harassment.

10. Don't spread gossip or rumors through email. It's bad enough when gossip is repeated on the telephone or in person, but email exponentially expands the number of people receiving such information.

11. Don't use email to replace telephone or personal contacts. It is important to maintain voice-to-voice and face-to-face relationships with the people we regularly deal with.

12. Don't send a message to your entire list unless the message applies to everyone on it.

Writing Better Reports

Most managers have to write reports on their activities or on special projects assigned by their bosses. Not only are such reports often critical to the success of a project, but the writer is also judged by what and how he or she has composed the report.

Denise, the purchasing manager of a furniture company, was appalled as she read and reread the report submitted by

Gary, her new assistant. She had asked him to investigate which of several types of forklift trucks might best suit their needs. His report was totally unsatisfactory. Not only was it superficial and lacking in clear analysis, but it also omitted some of the key points necessary to make a logical decision.

The study would have to be repeated and this would seriously delay obtaining the equipment required. This was Gary's first significant assignment and Denise was very disappointed. Perhaps she had made a mistake in promoting him to this job.

Many people short-change themselves by submitting poorly developed, poorly thought-out and even more poorly written reports. Why? Perhaps they believe that if they present the basic data, it is adequate. A good report must be far more than just basic information. It should enable the reader to obtain enough knowledge of the subject covered so that he or she can make whatever decisions are needed. It should also be written in a clear and concise manner so the reader does not have to cut through a jungle of irrelevancies to get to the key areas of concern.

Get All the Facts

Careful planning must go into a report. When Gary was given the assignment to obtain information about the equipment, all he did was request some literature from the three leading manufacturers, abstracted a few facts, and summarized his findings in the report.

To be more effective what should Gary have done?

1. *Define the Problem:* What is the objective of the report? Much time, effort and money is wasted by not knowing

what is really wanted. Gary should have asked Denise to clearly define what she wanted to know. Unless the report writer is aware of how the report will be used, he or she may spend more time on secondary aspects of the situation instead of the really important areas.

2. *Get the Facts:* Once the objectives are clear, try to get all the information needed. Gary was right in obtaining the manufacturers' literature, but he did not go far enough. In addition, he should have discussed the situation with the people in his company who would be using the forklifts to learn what special problems they face and how the new equipment might help them. He should have interviewed sales representatives of local distributors of these trucks and talk to other users of this type of equipment to determine their opinions and perhaps to learn of other equipment that might be more appropriate for his needs.

3. *Analyze the Facts:* Once the information is accumulated, all the facts should be assembled, correlated and analyzed by listing and comparing the advantages and limitations of each type of truck, it would be easier to determine how they fit into the overall objectives desired. If there is a clear-cut advantage of purchasing one product, Gary should recommend it. However, it is better to present more than one alternative so that Denise can make her own decision.

In assembling and analyzing facts, it is helpful to systematically keep information together and in order. One good technique is to open a computer folder for the project and set up files within it for each major category of the study. Supplement this by making up a folder or envelope to place appropriate sales literature, reports of interviews, printouts of cost figures and the like. Pre-sorting the facts this way instead of throwing all the material together and sorting them later can save many hours of sorting and assembling.

Writing the Report

Once all the data is collected, assembled and evaluated, the report can be written. An effective business report must be easy to read. Its language and form should be familiar to the person or persons who would be reading it. An engineer writing a report for a non-technical management group should try to couch the report in as non-technical language as the subject permits.

The report writer has an advantage when it is known what management expects in terms of language, details of content, graphic material and the like. Gary should know whether Denise prefers terse, precise reports or a great deal of detail. Does she want graphs and charts or does she prefer statistical tables giving exact figures?

Know the reader. Gear the report to his or her interest and desires. The report is written for that specific individual, so tailor it to that person's preferences.

Dale Carnegie

Report Format

Although there is no ideal report style, the format suggested in the following paragraphs has proved to be effective:

Briefly State the Problem: "As you requested, here is the

information on the brands and models of forklift trucks for our warehouse."

Summary and Recommendations: Present the summary and recommendations at the beginning of the report. This will enable the executives to get the key information at once. They do not have to wade through realms of detail to find out what is recommended.

Detailed Back-up: This is the meat of the report. It presents all the details that support the summary and recommendations. Charts, graphs and statistical tables may make the report more understandable. Photographs, where appropriate, can be very helpful.

Watch the language: Keep it clear and to the point. There is no need to use an elaborate, pedantic style. Relate the language to the interests and background of the reader. Good usage and choice words are important. A report can be terribly dull if there is no variety in sentence structure, no color in vocabulary, too many clichés or too banal a style of writing.

How long should a report be? Long enough to tell the whole story—and not one word longer. Avoid repetition. A common fault in report writing is stating the same idea over and over again in different words.

Submitting the Report

Before submitting the report, we should proofread it carefully. Even a good report loses credibility when it has spelling errors, poor grammatical structure, and sloppy typing. Figures should be checked carefully. Reread it before forwarding. If possible, have another person who is knowledgeable of the subject, read it. Make whatever changes that are needed.

Attention to the finer points of obtaining and presenting information and ideas in writing reports will result in your being recognized as a person who can successfully accomplish an assigned job. It will enhance your image in the eyes of your bosses as a person who can communicate ideas and present information effectively.

Sum and Substance

➤ Plan the message before writing one word.
➤ Be Complete, Concise, and Clear.
➤ The message will be clearer and more easily accepted if you write just the way you speak.
➤ Use charts, graphs, photographs, etc. where appropriate, to clarify or expand the message.
➤ Watch the grammar and spelling. Your writing style reflects your competence.
➤ Give as much attention to writing emails and text messages as to writing a standard letter.
➤ In writing a report, get all the facts, analyze the situation and understand what the person(s) to whom the report will be submitted really wants and how he or she wants it to be presented.

Appendix A

ABOUT DALE CARNEGIE &
ASSOCIATES, INC.

Founded in 1912, Dale Carnegie Training has evolved from one man's belief in the power of self-improvement to a performance-based training company with offices worldwide. It focuses on giving people in business the opportunity to sharpen their skills and improve their performance in order to build positive, steady, and profitable results.

Dale Carnegie's original body of knowledge has been constantly updated, expanded and refined through nearly a century's worth of real-life business experiences. The 160 Dale Carnegie Franchisees around the world use their training and consulting services with companies of all sizes, in all business segments to increase knowledge and performance. The result of this collective, global experience is an expanding reservoir of business acumen that our clients rely on to drive business results.

Headquartered in Hauppauge, New York, Dale Carnegie Training is represented in all 50 of the United States and over 75 countries. More than 2,700 instructors present Dale Carnegie Training programs in more than 25 languages. Dale Carnegie Training is dedicated to serving the business community worldwide. In fact, approximately 7 million people have completed Dale Carnegie Training.

Dale Carnegie Training emphasizes practical principles and processes by designing programs that offer people the knowledge, skills and practices they need to add value to their businesses. Connecting proven solutions with real-world challenges, Dale Carnegie Training is recognized internationally as the leader in bringing out the best in people.

Among the graduates of these programs are CEOs of major corporations, owners and managers of businesses of every size and every commercial and industrial activity, legislative and executive leaders of governments and countless individuals whose lives have been enriched by the experience.

In an ongoing global survey on customer satisfaction, 99 percent of Dale Carnegie Training graduates express satisfaction with the training they receive.

Appendix B

DALE CARNEGIE'S PRINCIPLES

Become a friendlier person

1. Don't criticize, condemn or complain.
2. Give honest, sincere appreciation.
3. Arouse in the other person an eager want.
4. Become genuinely interested in other people.
5. Smile.
6. Remember that a person's name is to that person the sweetest sound in any language.
7. Be a good listener. Encourage others to talk about themselves.
8. Talk in terms of the other person's interests.
9. Make the other person feel important—and do it sincerely.
10. To get the best of an argument—avoid it.
11. Show respect for the other person's opinion. Never tell a person he or she is wrong.
12. If you are wrong, admit it quickly, emphatically.

13. Begin in a friendly way.
14. Get the other person to say "yes" immediately.
15. Let the other person do a great deal of the talking.
16. Let the other person feel the idea is his or hers.
17. Try honestly to see things from the other person's point of view.
18. Be empathetic to the other person's ideas and desires.
19. Appeal to the nobler motives.
20. Dramatize your ideas.
21. Throw down a challenge.
22. Begin with praise and honest appreciation.
23. Call attention to people's mistakes indirectly.
24. Talk about your own mistakes before criticizing the other person.
25. Ask questions instead of giving direct orders.
26. Let the other person save face.
27. Praise the every slightest improvement. Be "hearty in your approbation and lavish in your praise."
28. Give the other person a fine reputation to live up to.
29. Use encouragement. Make the fault seem easy to correct.
30. Make the other person happy about doing the thing you suggest.

Fundamental Principles for Overcoming Worry

1. Live in "day—tight compartments."
2. How to face trouble:
   Ask yourself: "What is the worst that can possibly happen?"
3. Prepare to accept the worst.
4. Try to improve on the worst.
5. Remind yourself of the exorbitant price you can pay for worry in terms of your health.

Basic Techniques in Analyzing Worry

1. Get all the facts.
2. Weigh all the facts—then come to a decision.
3. Once a decision is reached, act!
4. Write out and answer the following questions:
   - What is the problem?
   - What are the causes of the problem?
   - What are the possible solutions?
   - What is the best possible solution?

Break the Worry Habit Before It Breaks You

1. Keep busy.
2. Don't fuss about trifles.
3. Use the law of averages to outlaw your worries.
4. Cooperate with the inevitable.
5. Decide just how much anxiety a thing may be worth and refuse to give it more.
6. Don't worry about the past.

Cultivate a Mental Attitude That Will Bring You Peace and Happiness

1. Fill your mind with thoughts of peace, courage, health and hope.
2. Never try to get even with your enemies.
3. Expect ingratitude.
4. Count your blessings—not your troubles.
5. Do not imitate others.
6. Try to profit from your losses.
7. Create happiness for others.